Hin

Hindsights

Ten Meetings of Minds

Liam Ó Murchú

Gill & Macmillan

Gill & Macmillan Ltd
Hume Avenue, Park West, Dublin 12
with associated companies throughout the world
www.gillmacmillan.ie

0 7171 3126 2

Design by Vermillion
Print origination by Andy Gilsenan, Dublin
Printed by ColourBooks Ltd, Dublin

This book is typeset in Bembo 12 on 14.

A CIP catalogue record for this book is available from the
British Library.

5 4 3 2 1

Contents

Preface

Some of the encounters recorded here go back a long time. The little 5-year-old atop his brother's shoulders in a victory parade welcoming hurling hero Jack Lynch back to Cork in 1934 becomes Robbie Burns's 'chile amang ye takin' notes' for Dr Noel Browne during the Mother and Child row in 1950; thirty years on, he will have both those men sitting beside him in a television talk-show. By then the Irish language has become central to his life. It is the living link with most of the others who come into the picture here, a language learnt in Christian Brothers' schools, though not a word of it was spoken by his own people for generations.

It is the reason he comes to know most of them—and, with some, more than to know, to love: Tomás Ó Fiaich, Seán Ó Riada, Siobhán McKenna, Cyril Cusack. Dark clouds gathered over the lives of others in later times: Éamonn Casey and Charles Haughey. But, through success and failure, hope and hopelessness, there is always a present which is the heart and centre of all our lives. The past is past and cannot be remade; the future is not yet and may not ever be. What I tell here is told as it is happening, with occasional ominous signs and portents of what is to come.

With all ten names there were surely good times and bad, times of hope and times of despair, times of success and times of failure. But as I—that 'chile amang ye takin' notes'—was seeing things, through each and every one of them there was much idealism, commitment and dedication to the life of Ireland.

Even the biggest and best among us is but a spark in a never-ending fire, a fleeting moment in the mainstream of eternity, 'a poor player that struts and frets his hour upon the stage and then is heard no more.' This is the part of one such poor player in the times recorded here. Slight though it be, it may yet be worth a glance before being blown away like a puff of smoke or an autumn leaf falling to the ground. These few pages, these memories of a small part in large lives, may serve to show aspects and features of those lives which might not otherwise be known.

A final word: one's memory of times past can sometimes be faulty. For such inaccuracies as may be here, be kind enough to excuse because of age and the passing years— both factors about which, alas, there is not much I can do!

Fiery Particle

DR NOEL BROWNE

It is the month of January 1948 and I am a callow youth, all of 18 years old. Callow I may be, but stupid I am not. In proof of this, I have got myself what many think is a prime job in the Irish Civil Service. I am posted to the Department of Health in the Custom House, which I quickly learn is the masterpiece of someone called Gandon, built at a time, some century and a half before, when Ireland briefly had a government of her own. In January 1948 Ireland will shortly have a new government of her own, her first ever Coalition. In that government the affairs of the Department of Health will be entrusted to a young doctor who had not alone never been in government before, but had never been in politics at all. His name is Noel Browne.

A Health Act of the previous year, put through by the outgoing Fianna Fáil, gave clear evidence that they were serious about getting to grips with the graver health problems of the time which had been neglected in favour of more urgent matters during the 1939–45 war. They included tuberculosis, a plague which could, and did, wipe out whole families, and a Mother and Child Scheme to deal with alarmingly high levels of maternal and infant mortality. Those projects, and others envisaged in the new Act, would all have come along in time. But, suddenly, that January the unexpected happened: Fianna Fáil was out, the Coalition was in, and with it this anonymous young doctor sweeps into the mainstream of Irish political life.

In setting the scene at the outset of that life, it is relevant to say this: administration is a skill; the public communication of ideas is a skill; and negotiation and conciliation between conflicting viewpoints are skills. They are skills that the callow youth I am does not possess. More to the point, they are skills which his 32-year-old lord and master does not possess in any great measure either. A time is coming when he will sorely need them.

The Hospitals Construction section where I go to work becomes the powerhouse of the new health scene. Within weeks of Browne's arrival, a seven year building programme is up and going, with big new hospitals and sanatoria being planned all over the place. There is a new architectural nerve-centre headed by a workaholic, Norman White, and staffed by a coterie of eager beavers, all alive with architectural brainwaves.

The sanatoria building programme will be the direct responsibility of the department itself, not of some lethargic local authority moving at a snail's pace, to get things done. With Browne, nothing moves at a snail's pace; everything is done and done fast. With his lightning-charge attached, we do not live by the normal rules: for one thing, he arrives in his Custom House office driving his own MG sports car— some garda driver has a cushy time of it in those days! Once in, he goes straight to his progress maps—huge wall charts with all the works in progress in different colours at their various stages of development. Nor is it just hospitals and sanatoria: old country mansions that come on the market are bought up and converted for use as TB isolation units; out-of-work payments are made to those affected to lure them into care—anything and everything that will help his purpose. No opportunity is lost, no cost too great. His dynamic is infectious. Large or small, high up or low down, we are all caught up in it. Few of us know then what his driving force is: it will be years later, when all the Mother and Child controversy which will engulf him has passed and his own effective political life is over, that he does a 'self-portrait' on RTÉ one night in which, walking along the banks of a canal in Ballinrobe, he tells the story of how he came to live in this small and backward place. After his father died, their mother brought the family there because it had a workhouse, still functioning, where she would stand in the queue for hours waiting for free food. He stops and chokes as he tells this grim story, remembering that, in short order, first his father, then his mother, then his older sister who took over the family after them, all died of TB in the same way. I see then, as I have not seen before, what the source of that driving force within him is—the same drive, the same loyalty to his own, which is the story of the Irish down through the generations.

This is the Noel Browne we come to know and love. He is a refined and cultured man, a man of slow and hesitant speech, sometimes almost a whisper, but carrying some deep inner conviction. He certainly shows no signs of the flat, elongated vowels of the Irish midlands where he grew up; it is more the speech of the exclusive Jesuit Beaumont College in England, and later Trinity, where, through the goodness of rich Irish patrons, he had been sent. During the three years he will spend in the Custom House, he will find time to re-learn his primary school Irish; in the darkly varnished corridors of the ministers' quarters we frequently see his tutor, Seosamh Ó Cadhain, brother of the author Máirtín Ó Cadhain, sitting patiently outside his door, waiting for some urgent conference to break up so that he can go in. From this he will with time develop the nuance and idiom of native Connemara speech; but even then there will always be a substratum of the English public school.

His dress, his voice, his Greek-god face and long hair—at a time when long hair was not the fashion—all make for a debonair and exceptionally elegant young man. Anyone who saw Kurt Hatfield in *The Picture of Dorian Grey* knows what he looked like.

He is not always the aloof Greek god. At times he will come out with a light, whimsical touch, extremely charming to the casual observer, though probably infuriating to someone at the receiving end. Once, when he has finished a meeting with a deputation from the midlands at which I have taken notes, he is standing in the ministers' room pouring himself a glass of water from a carafe. His departmental secretary, Pádraig Ó Cinnéide, a grey-suited, grey-faced man, asks him how he has got on.

'Fine,' he replies. 'They were very persuasive, especially Deputy Flanagan who made a strong case for a grant of 100 per cent.'

The grant was for the renovation of the Mountmellick County Home and the deputy was Oliver Flanagan, the one-man party of 'Monetary Reform' some years before, but latterly a member of Fine Gael, though a constant thorn in their side.

'I hope, Minister, you didn't give it to them,' Secretary Ó Cinnéide says.

'I gave them two-thirds.'

'But you can't. Fifty per cent is the norm. You can't exceed that. Word will get out, every county home in the country will want it. The Hospitals Trust Fund cannot afford it.'

'I know that perfectly well, Mr Kennedy,' he blithely responds. Then, pausing, he raises the glass and the bold-boy look comes into his eyes. 'One of these days even the Minister for Health is going to realise that his Hospitals Trust Fund won't last for ever.'

It is a far cry from this to a moment close on thirty years later when I will have him as the principal guest on my television programme, 'Trom agus Éadrom'. Remembering the elegant and sophisticated young man he then was, I ask if he would like to hear what people like me thought of him in those years. Reluctantly, he says yes, knowing full well that I am going to tell him anyway.

'You struck us', I say, 'as the picture of the gracious, elegant, educated ENGLISH gentleman!'—a comment which, some time shortly afterwards, has Taoiseach Jack Lynch telling me that it was the one and only time he had ever seen Noel Browne openly laugh!

This Hospitals Trust Fund has been built up from the proceeds of the Irish Sweepstakes over many years. It is the financial powerhouse for his seven year hospitals and sanatoria building programme. But, though Browne is the minister responsible for its disbursal, there are other interested parties, most notably the Department of Finance, guardian of the national purse. Browne wants to use the fund down to the last penny in the interests of the nation's health. What else is it there for but that? he petulantly asks. But, amounting as it does to several millions—small by the standards of later times, but huge then—it constitutes a large part of the nation's external assets invested in gilt-edged securities abroad. Hence in the Scrooge-like view of the finance mandarins it is to be kept and hoarded, not frittered away on a non-productive sector like health. It is an uneven contest. The populace is massively with Browne in his fight against TB. The mandarins lose.

So he drives on, his Department of Health becoming what Seán Lemass in later times will call a 'developmental agency', when speaking of his own brain-children, the IDA, Bord Fáilte, Córas Tráchtála and the Shannon Free Airport Development Company. Freed from the rigidity of civil service controls, such agencies could press on more speedily with the business in hand. Browne inculcates this sense of freedom to innovate, to improvise, in his whole staff—doctors, architects and civil servants. We are all caught up in it. There is a job of major national importance to be done; and with frenetic zeal he strains every nerve and muscle to do it.

Later, with hindsight, it will be argued by his adversaries that the huge expenditure on new sanatoria was unnecessary because the miracle drugs shortly to come on the scene will eradicate TB. But in 1948, when his sanatoria programme was launched, those drugs did not exist. Could he who had seen the ravages of TB at first hand in his own life and, later, that of his wife, be blamed for not foreseeing that development? Could he be blamed for pressing on with tackling, with the only resources he had, a disease which was killing thousands year by year?

It is at the height of one of his emotive and high-flown verbal flights against the finance mandarins that I hear him make a remark one day which, though clearly well meant, will certainly be later interpreted as one of his wilder over-statements. If put in the scales beside each other, he says, the whole of the Hospitals Trust Fund could not outweigh the value of one single life. It is the language of the idealist—one could see that the word 'fanatic' might more readily come to conservative lips. To this 18-year old, to all the others around him, what it showed was a burning concern for people's suffering, a concern which in turn is surely at the core of the second of the two great commandments by which we are enjoined to live—'Love thy neighbour.' When his time of trouble comes, as it will, few of those doctrinaire Christians who so vehemently opposed him could claim to have given as shining an example of how that commandment should be kept.

We have half a century to go to the years of the Celtic Tiger in that dim and distant past when that seven year building programme of his is being launched; but there is at the time the same bustling and infectious energy about, which those who survive to the Celtic Tiger time will know. This is perhaps best characterised by the brightly coloured booklet he commissions to publicise the works in progress and how they are affecting national morale. *Ireland Is Building, Come Home and Work* is its title. He is greatly helped in this by an unlikely PR man—a role unheard of in public life then—Aodh de Blacam, 'Roddy the Rover' of the *Irish Press*. He had written a fine critique of literary work in the Irish language, *Gaelic Literature Surveyed*—in some ways a companion book to *The Hidden Ireland* by Daniel Corkery. He and Corkery shared the same pride in cultural nationalism, derived from the early years of the Gaelic League and the Young Ireland movement of Thomas Davis, whose path to freedom was the slogan, 'Educate that you may be free.' When Browne brings him to the Department of Health, he proves to be a publicist of considerable insight in this exciting new phase in Irish life. As well as *Ireland Is Building*, he fixes a weekly slot on the Radio Éireann 'Hospitals Requests' programme presented by Éamonn Andrews. With this, the public are informed about what is being planned and kept up to date on the progress of the building programme.

Another innovation is an attractive, brightly coloured stand at the RDS Spring Show, with maps, artists' impressions and other publicity material. So the message is spread: the monster TB is being confronted; from now on there will be less weeping above the coffins of beloved sons and daughters, sisters and brothers, mothers and fathers. After Browne's departure three years later, 'Roddy the Rover' is shafted and is never heard of again. That is a loss and a great pity. He is the forerunner of all that glitz and glamour set which, light years from then, will come to be known as 'spin doctors'; though to do him justice, one may doubt whether any of the later breed had the vision, the national spirit and the cultural enlightenment of that patriotic man.

De Blacam belongs to what one may call the first phase of Browne's ministerial tenure. Another writer, Michael Mulvihill, who will become his private secretary, belongs to the second. But there is a whole world of difference between those two phases: in the first, up to the middle of 1950, the emphasis is on TB and its eradication, on hospitals and sanatoria construction, and on the attendant publicity this entailed; in the second, which will last for the remainder of his time, the theme that will take precedence and dominate the whole subsequent discourse on health is 'Mother and Child'.

With the publication of a White Paper on this subject, the forward-looking dynamic atmosphere which characterised his tenure up to that seems to change—to be replaced by one of argument, contention and a highly combative dialectic which will bring the storm clouds closer day by day. In due course it will develop, in one manifestation, into an endless correspondence in the 'Letters to the Editor' columns of *The*

Irish Times under the title 'The Liberal Ethic'. Several weighty intellects get involved in this, chief among them a Galway University Franciscan academic, Fr Felim Ó Briain, and one from Trinity College, Owen Sheehy Skeffington. It is all high theology and philosophy, with much high-flown gouts of verbiage being thrown about—among them 'the doctrine of subsidiary function' which we readers are meant to interpret as one of the main reasons why Browne's free-for-all Mother and Child scheme is contrary to Church teaching. This is not the place, nor am I the person, to go into the pros and cons of his famous scheme. In the years that follow, this will be done exhaustively—exhaustingly?—in all branches of the media. But perhaps I may say this much: the two or three 'offending' sections in his White Paper could have easily been amended to achieve the substance of what he had in mind without causing the 'offence'.

In effect, in legislation which will eventually emerge, they *will* be amended, pretty well to the satisfaction of all. But as the scene is unfolding, with what the doctrinaire Catholic hierarchy is saying—and the even more doctrinaire higher echelons of a medical profession hell bent on maintaining its preserve on patients' fees under the guise of medical ethics— Browne rapidly finds himself cornered by two of the most powerful estates in the land. And he has neither the guile nor, let it be plainly stated, the administrative and negotiatory skills to pick his way through the morass to the *terra firma* of political acceptability which might have seen him safely home.

From then on the same committed, frenetic energy which went into the marvellous developmental years will become steadily eroded, sometimes in half-ridiculous pursuits aimed at scoring small technical or moral points. We on the ground are set the task of seeking out texts on social teaching which will give crumbs of comfort against the hierarchy's case; while less than theological texts are scrutinised for proof that the official medical associations do not represent the majority of doctors at all. So for days on end I find myself in the National Library checking medical names in the telephone directory against names published in the directories of the medical associations to prove that they do not represent the whole medical fraternity! Compared to the marvellous practical dynamic of the TB years, this is more in the snail's pace of *Waiting for Godot*!

It even begins to show in his outward appearance. From being that elegant, debonair, self-assured young man we all so much admired, Browne now begins to develop a sharper, more abrasive edge. A personal letter in the spidery, nun-like hand of Archbishop McQuaid, or a public one in the columns of *The Irish Times* by a Dr McPolin, one of the medical side's more vociferous protagonists, will engender a fury of ill-suppressed rage. Some of this can lead to internal rows and differences with fine people who, while trying to help their minister through bureaucratic and hierarchical quagmires, somehow get bogged down in the process and end up being sidelined because they will not toe the official line. Some of the story is told in Dr Jim Deeny's fine book, *To Care and To Cure*—though that ebullient and delightful man, himself sidelined, will go on to fight, not just one, but many another day.

It is into this second phase of Noel Browne's ministerial life that Michael Mulvihill comes as private secretary. Michael, a splendid writer, had had TB himself and will go on to write a fine play about it and about life in the 'consumption' wards—*A Sunset Touch*.

Much later, after he has long left the civil service, I will be able to help in getting him taken on by Maxwell Sweeney as a contributor to 'Sunday Miscellany', where his sonorous, high-flown prose will always be touched with an endearing, if equally high-flown, 'hauteur' when addressing his favourite themes—the life and landmarks of his boyhood years in Kerry and Kilkenny, Shakespeare's plays and the poetry of Yeats, Tennyson and Robert Browning. Some of the phraseology in Browne's speeches around the time of the Mother and Child controversy will certainly bear the marks of Michael's florid, declamatory style. But there is no doubting the bond that exists between the two men, a bond cemented by their common experience of seeing at first hand the deaths of good friends in the TB wards. It is from this that Michael takes the theme and title of his fine play:

Just when you're nearest, there's a sunset touch,
The murmur of a flower-bell, someone's death,
A Chorus-ending from Euripides.

The Mother and Child story, from Browne's point of view, will be told years later in his personal memoir, *Against the Tide*. The first half of this book, about his childhood and growing years in Athlone and Ballinrobe, surely ranks among the finest, most moving pieces of autobiography to have ever come out of Ireland. Predictably, perhaps, when he gets on to the controversial years, he is on somewhat shakier ground. Who would not be, bearing in mind the mauling he has endured, not alone from open adversaries, but from some who had been colleagues and close friends?

When he finally leaves office in 1951, there are people

who had been close to him who weep openly. Jack Darby, the one perhaps most closely involved with him in the Mother and Child scheme, comes back down to us on the ground floor of the Custom House, his eyes still red, unable to speak. That is the kind of loyalty, love even, which Noel Browne in his time has evoked.

A time will come when all this will be in the dim and distant past. By then Noel Browne will be dead. By all the laws, having passed the biblical three score and ten, I may not have all that long to go myself. So, with the benefit of age and hindsight, there are perhaps one or two things I may say. The first is that, had he not been the fiery particle he was, he might have handled things a great deal better. The wilful and headstrong young man who had so sure-footedly spearheaded a successful campaign against one of the worst plagues the country had ever known, was also wilful and headstrong when it came to treading the less sure-footed paths of diplomacy and political life. The highly privileged years of Beaumont and Trinity College left him ill-equipped to deal with the authoritarian stance of Irish churchmen who, in those years, had the unquestioned allegiance of the vast majority of their people in whatever line they took; more ill-equipped still to deal with the stance of an entrenched and self-interested medical establishment which knew where its advantage lay and was quick to read the signs when that advantage seemed threatened.

So when, in his White Paper, he speaks about 'the education of women in respect of motherhood', what he is talking about are the ordinary, common sense things an expectant mother should do during pregnancy—good diet, no smoking, a modicum of exercise and rest; certainly not the ghoulish interpretations which are put upon the phrase by his adversaries—mass contraception, abortion and the plethora of sex options which have become so familiar to us since. It is all, in Hamlet's phrase, a matter of 'words, words, words'; but then 'words, words, words' could have changed it. If he—and, assuming that he himself was at all persuadable, the people about him—had been able to come up with a form of words to encapsulate the substance of what he had in mind without the 'offence', then this aspect of the crisis need never have happened; and, in due course, would have been seen for what it was, a bout of juvenile shadow-boxing where all concerned were essentially of the same mind but could not seem to find a form of words to express it.

Or, again, when his White Paper spoke of a 'Free For All Mother and Child Service', he must have known that that did not state accurately what he wanted at all; rather, he envisaged a service that would be free for those *who could not afford to pay*. This was a wholly different concept, one which could not possibly have been objected to by those social theorists of the 'doctrine of subsidiary function', according to which the state should not intervene except by way of subsidiary aid to families too poor to pay for the service themselves.

The proof of all this will come a few years later when Fianna Fáil minister, Dr Jim Ryan, sits down with the 'Free For All Mother and Child Committee', comprising well-known activists like Peadar O'Donnell, Ruairí Roberts, Louie Bennett and Labour senator Miss Davidson; and, with those skills of negotiation and conciliation I mentioned earlier, will quietly bring them around to his point of view.

By a strange irony, it comes to pass that I have a ringside seat at this too, being note-taker at the meeting during which the debate is conducted. Step by quiet step, Ryan, a big, bumbling but skilful old man who had tended the wounded socialist James Connolly in the GPO in 1916 and never forgot it, will bring them through it. By 'free for all' do they mean—these are his very words—'free for the rich company director's wife living in a big house in Foxrock, with two cars in the driveway?' No, they vehemently deny, they certainly do not mean that.

'Well, then, that says we must have a means test, a limit above which you can reasonably expect people to pay for themselves. What should that be? You tell me.'

The figure (it's £600—put that in your Celtic Tiger pipe and smoke it!) is readily agreed, but there is more.

'That may be all right for a first or a second child,' he says, 'but what about a third, fourth or fifth? Six hundred pounds wouldn't be fair then.'

So a clause is put in to cover that. But there are still problems even after that. If a mother is severely ill, for example, and needs lengthy hospitalisation and costly drugs, that kind of expense could wreck a family, even one comparatively well off. So provision is made for that. Lastly, there could be 'special circumstances', things unforeseen by any of the above; so an exceptional hardship clause is put in to cover those.

It is all there, down to the last dot and comma, in section 15 of the Health Act 1953; and the 'Free For All Mother and Child Committee', who had come to the meeting breathing fire and brimstone because Browne was shafted, leave it completely satisfied.

There is a sequel. One night many years later, driving into town with him in his very old but very stylish sports car, I put it to him that he had gone into the Division Lobby in Dáil Éireann when the Committee Stage of that Bill was going through and voted for section 15. How could he bring himself to do that, when he had brought himself and a government down on some of those very issues a few years earlier? I have clearly touched a sore point and he becomes very tetchy, very cross with me. It occurs to me then that, with the years, he may have come to suspect, as I have, that the idea of making someone a senior minister on his very first day in the House may not have been the wisest thing for a new government to do!

It all happened, as I say, a long time ago. Noel Browne is now dead; most of those close to him in both government and department are dead too. Though half a century has passed, there are, as we know, still gaps and deficiencies in the health services. No doubt, there will always be. The millions spent on his building programmes are billions now; the workforce he strove so hard to recruit and motivate is but a mite of what it has now become.

One small relaxation from the gruelling work routines he lived through in those years will later stand to him—those Irish language grinds he did with Seosamh Ó Cadhain, squeezed in between scores of more pressing claims. Those will bear fruit years later when he takes himself off to live in Baile na hAbhann in the Connemara Gaeltacht. There, I am happy to read in his widow's memoir, *Thanks for the Tea, Mrs Browne*, he was very much at home. Sometimes, in those years, I sail past him, tacking up the sound at Rossaveal in his small yacht, while I and my children in a smaller one are tacking down! He has come a long way from the workhouse in Ballinrobe by then, an even longer one from the ivy leagues of Beaumont and Trinity College. But along part of that way he left his mark upon the life of Ireland. Whatever his later failures and misfortunes, in those brief few years he took by the throat the unassailable monster which was devouring the flower and youth of Ireland. For that he has the thanks of many living who owe their lives to him; and of the dead who, but for him, would have died long before their time.

A Neighbour's Child

JACK LYNCH

More than a dozen years before the name Noel Browne ever crossed my line of vision, I had heard the name of Jack Lynch. The first time I heard it was when our local hurling heroes, the Christian Brothers 'North Mon.' beat Rockwell College in the final of the Harty Cup. There was Jack, above the crowd on a horse-drawn dray draped in the blue and white colours of the school, with the other stalwarts of the team around him. He was not the only one aloft. For so was I, all of 5, and in danger of being trampled on by the thousands who turned out to greet them in Glanmire Station, atop the shoulders of my big brother, Ken, who was a class ahead of him in the North Mon.

It is a night I will remember. Molly Owens, matriarch fruit-dealer and amazon-in-chief, has bonfires burning at the top of Shandon Street near the school, an honour-fest she puts on whenever her great hero Éamon de Valera comes to Cork. There is a torchlight procession up through the city with, out front, the band of the Butter Exchange from beside the Lynches' house under Shandon; they are our local symphony and philharmonic orchestras all rolled into one! Up McCurtain Street they go, into Patrick Street, then on to the Grand Parade. From a hastily erected platform there, great rabble-rousing speeches are made and the game is played all over again. Every time the cup is raised, the crowd goes wild with delight and the heroes are toasted again and again—team captain 'Smiler' Riordan, 'Cooper' Moylan, Sonny Buckley, Frank Casey, the Lynch brothers, Jack and Finbarr. Some of them have their heads swathed in bandages, for us youngsters the stuff of hero-worship: 'Home they brought their warrior dead'! Small wonder that 'Blood and bandages!' with 'Up the rebels!' will be the war-cry in Cork hurling for years to come.

Forty years later Jack Lynch will be a name known throughout the length and breadth of Ireland; but from that night on it is a name that is known throughout the length and breadth of Cork. Hurling and politics, which came first? He is in no doubt about that. In a television programme I do with him years later, he tells me that from his hurling and football days he had learnt all he ever needed to know for political life: the cut and thrust, the fire and brimstone, the will to win, the even greater will to put up with it when you lose.

Five years after that Harty Cup win, he is in Croke Park playing against Kilkenny in the 'thunder and lightning All-Ireland' of 1939. By then I am 10 years old and can run fast; but when the thunderous skies open and the lightning strikes, there is nowhere to run to, so we just stand there and get drowned. But it is not the deluge that drowns us so much as the killer instinct of the Kilkenny 'cats' as they drive ball after ball with magnetic ease between the Cork posts. Cork are two points down in the dying seconds when Jack Lynch lobs in a lovely ball to Micka Brennan, lying loose on the wing. For speed and pace, Micka had earlier kicked off his boots and now, as he swings at the dropping ball to finish it to the net, he slips on the sodden grass and barely touches it to clip it over the bar. Not for the first or the last time, the 'cats' have it. And on the train home to Cork that night, I hear old men mutter into their glasses of flat porter words of hope for a new resurrection: 'No matter, boys, we'll rise again!'

And rise they do. Two years later they are back in Croke Park, as they will be in all five years following, including 1945 when the hurlers lose but the footballers win. In the last of those years, Jack Lynch wins his sixth in a row All-Ireland medal. By now his name and fame have gone far and wide, but as yet there is no hint of politics. That is how things are when that same big brother Ken, who had me on his shoulders in 1934, comes home one night to tell our mother that Jack Lynch is standing for election.

'Why wouldn't he, the decent boy?' Mother says. 'And he'll get in too, top of the poll.'

'But he's going up for de Valera,' Ken tells her.

Now, for Mother, de Valera is the devil incarnate. He started the Civil War, conducted it single handed; before that, he had the gall to tell the Brits to get out—the good benefactors who had given her and her likes the 'separation money' when their soldier-men were away at the wars.

'The Lynches were always decent people,' she stoutly declares. 'There's no way that decent boy will have anything to do with *him.*'

And true to her word, in election after election to her dying day, she goes out and votes No. 1 Jack Lynch, never for an instant doubting that the 'decent boy' will ever do anything but what is right.

That is the kind of esteem in which Jack Lynch was held in Cork—and the kind of blind fidelity that will see him clock up 20,000 votes in Cork North Central at the height of his political life.

The story of our families' association goes back even further than that, for our Uncle Jimmy had this coal store at 'Bob and Joan' under Shandon, near where the Lynches lived. Bob and Joan were two effigies in the garden representing the poor boys and girls who were taken into a 'Bird's Nest' type orphanage there. Uncle Jimmy was always telling us about the titanic games of hurling that were played up and down the narrow alley there and, when the day turned wet, continued in the basement of their house. Some of the players will later become fabled names in the story of Cork hurling. All around them there are the close-knit warrens of lanes and alleys off Shandon Street and Blackpool, a throbbing and vibrant pulse of life, squalid and fetid with the loves and labours of thousands of Cork's poor. So when that youngest of the Lynch boys, Jack, runs down from 'Bob and Joan' to buy 'two pair of bread' from the bakery of Ormonde and Aherne on Shandon Street, he will run as fast as his legs will carry him to get away from the ravenous urchins of 'Shandon-a' and 'Blarney-a', who would grab it from him and rend it apart with houndstooth relish, for—no blasphemy intended—it would truly be manna from heaven.

Their mother, a kindly woman with a squad of children of her own, surely had enough to do with the small means they had without caring for other people's woes; but still, on the bitter cold days when the wind blew up the river from Pope's Quay, she would send one of the boys down with a 'ponny' of hot tea for Uncle Jimmy. This is the scene in which young Jack Lynch grew up. Fifty years on, when the latter-day reformers came hectoring him about the need for reforms to help the poor, did they not know that he had seen more poverty before he was 10 than they would see in a lifetime?

It will be a long time after those early childhood years before I meet him face to face. This is when the North Monastery Past Pupils Union is re-established in 1946 after a lapse for the war years—and I am nominated to represent the 'new boys'. We meet in a room in the Metropole Hotel—it is the first time this improver has ever been through its doors! What confronts me when I go in is a collection of what seems to me to be very old men. Bearing in mind that I am all of 17, some might have gone near enough to qualifying for that description: Henry Weldon, the president, is 40-odd—to me, a ripe old age. Even older is Gus Healy, later a TD and, after Lynch's landslide victory of 1977, Chairman of Fianna Fáil.

Others there are in their mid to late 30s, greybeards to this beardless 17-year old. Then Jack Lynch arrives. He is now at the peak of his hurling fame. But he too is clearly getting on: he is smoking a pipe—a sure sign of advancing age; he has an incipient bald patch; he is wearing a fine Crombie overcoat which only the rich—and ageing—can afford! So may the young be blinded by the folly of youth when confronted with the folly of age!

Irreverent as it may seem, I begin to see images of the child Jesus in the temple, with the scribes and elders about him 'hearing them and answering their questions'. A later, less celestial image is that of Peter O'Toole in *The Ruling Class* who, coming into his earldom at a young age, enters the House of Lords for the first time, where what confronts him is a galaxy of old fogies with cobwebs and spiders crawling all over them! It is an image flattering to neither the House of Lords nor the North Monastery Past Pupils Union. But then it is an image created by a member of the '17-year-old Ruling Class OK!'

Nor is it helped by the fact that the first item on the

agenda is the date for what is to be their annual dress dance. Now, to us, a dress dance is a highly prestigious affair; further, at that time and place, no one but the snobs of our local 'Nob Hill'(Montenotte) ever get to be within an ass's roar of one. Yet here we are, past pupils of the proletarian North Mon., earnestly discussing the date and details for this main event in our activities year. Struck dumb as I am by this apostasy, though normally a voluble youth, not a single syllable passes my lips. Nor is that all: for when dates are being discussed, with diaries out on the table to check them, one of those present—was it that scholarly yet affable man Tadhg Carey, later UCC President, then just back from England to take up a mathematics lectureship?—says he cannot make it for a month from now because he has to go back to England to 'pick up his gear'.

The phrase sticks. This is the first generation of post-independence working-class Ireland, where formal dress-wear is thought to be the mark of an effete and degenerate aristocracy—a foreign aristocracy at that—an idea subliminally nurtured in us by a description in common use for aficionados of the 'Castle Catholic' regime as 'Lucht na bheistí bána' (the crowd with the white waistcoats). So when I come back to report the proceedings to my own teenage constituency, including the 'gear' phrase, one of them comes out with what is surely a most unusual idea for dress-wear.

'Christ Almighty,' he says, 'don't tell me they're going to go to a dress dance in their hurling jerseys!'

In the currency of the time, it would have been no more incredible than that we ragamuffin boys could have risen to the price of a dress suit. Little did we think that a time would come when turning out in a team jersey would be quite an acceptable way to pass the fashion test. Or that an as yet unsighted animal known as a 'Celtic Tiger' would strip us of the last vestiges of our penury and leave us, not just without a Christian Brothers Past Pupils dress-dance to go to, but without a Christian Brother in sight at all!

I get to know other members of the Lynch clan long before I get to know Jack himself. His first cousin, Tadhg Lynch, is my classmate in the North Mon. And, coming down Mulgrave Road from the school like Eevil Kneevil on our bikes, we sometimes meet his uncle, Jack's father, walking home to the house at Bob and Joan. His wife had died many years before, leaving the younger members, including Jack, largely in the care of an aunt who lived near by. He is a silent, lonely man in his black hat and overcoat walking slowly to the big empty house which had once been so full of life. He will die as he lived, quietly and silently, on the footpath on Mulgrave Road, with Shandon, his goodly neighbour, leaving him in little doubt for whom the bell tolled.

The fact that Tadhg is a first cousin gives him a familial access which none of us outsiders has. This is especially the case with his cousin Charlie, a much-loved priest in the city. Like all the Lynch boys, he is a staunch Glen Rovers hurling man; and, to relieve him of the tension coming up to a big match, he will sometimes join us during the summer months in our swimming-place up the river at Carrigrohane. There, as the long, languid afternoons pass, he will sit around with us, discussing the great affairs of the world as we experts see them from the epicentre of Cork.

One such day, the conversation turns to the subject of sexual relations, on which we are keen to learn what the position of the one true Church might be. Cousin Tadhg, being on the inside track, may make bolder than the rest of us in such delicate matters and eventually comes out with the straight question.

'What would you say now, Father Charlie? Would you say now that it's a sin to kiss a girl?'

The Reverend Lynch, knowing he has the attention of young, virile males, hums and haws while he cogitates on how best to respond to this theological conundrum. Seeing him vacillate, cousin Tadhg comes to the rescue with his own *ex cathedra* pronouncement.

'I suppose what you're goin' to say, Charlie, is that it has to be a sin. Sure, if it wasn't a sin, wouldn't we be all doin' it?'

In the light of more knowing times, one may wonder at the profundity of this nugget of moral theology; but to us then it is by no means an outlandish view. Now, more than half a century later, not alone is it not a sin to kiss a girl—or a boy or a man either for that matter—but it is not a sin to do pretty well anything else one pleases, sin having been abolished and replaced by a more comfortable culture which says that sin, and what goes with it, are governed by one rule and one rule only: the 'I'm-all-right-Jack rule, OK!'

In later times, I will meet Father Charlie whenever he comes to Dublin to visit another brother, Finbarr. By then Finbarr is working with us in the Department of Health in the Custom House; and, though a dozen years older—he was a classmate of my brother Ken in the North Mon.—we become good friends. However, unlike most of the 'one-way ticket' fraternity who settle down in Dublin, Finbarr never takes to the role of permanent exile at all. So, when a job comes up in Cork, he applies for and gets it. At that time he is a higher executive and would certainly go higher if he stayed; the job in Cork is at a lower level and is lesser paid. But Cork being what it is, it is confidently rumoured that his brother Jack, then a minister, has used his political influence to throw the balance in his brother's favour. If so, it must be the one and only time in the history of the public service when political influence was used in order to get someone demoted!

So, with Finbarr gone from the Custom House, and me gone shortly afterwards to RTÉ, we are pretty well out of touch except when we meet during summer holidays in Ballyferriter. There, one day, while having a drink together in Dónall Ó Catháin's pub, someone who was a classmate of Jack in the North Mon. joins us. He quotes a newspaper report on the previous day's Dáil proceedings in which George Colley, then Minister for Education, is lecturing the Labour Party on the proper role for socialists in the new Ireland; and winds up by saying, 'If there were a proper Labour Party in this country, I would belong to it.'

'That's the kind of visionary leadership the country needs,' the former classmate tells Finbarr. 'And it's the reason Colley will be Taoiseach one day—and your brother never will.'

Within a few short years Jack Lynch *is* Taoiseach, with a large majority over Colley, who insisted on putting it to a vote, though the dogs of the street knew Lynch would win. So much for the predictions of all expert hurlers on the ditch!

That is 1967; Jack Lynch is then 50 years old. The glory years of hurling and football are behind him. Now, a new set of glory years are ahead. From then on he will become familiar with the sound and fury of new band parades, new addresses of welcome, new 'plaudits of the multitudes'. But he never loses the common touch; he will still remember the 'Uncle Jimmys' all over the country, wherever he goes; he will remember too that sturdy youth in short pants with 'two pair of bread' from Ormonde and Aherne's under his oxter, hotly pursued by other sturdy youths from the lanes off

'Shandon-a' and 'Blarney-a' as he races to the safe haven of his home. Did the prophet in Ó Catháin's who admired the socialist rhetoric of George Colley have any notion of the far more bred-in-the-bone socialism of someone who had grown up like that?

My first assignment in RTÉ was that of editor of Irish language programmes and among the programmes I launch is 'Iarphroinn', an after-dinner chat-show. ('Iarphroinn' means literally that, after a meal.) The language is a very unfavoured child in RTÉ at this time, with producers jumping into presses to get away from having to work on programmes that are low audience, low facilities and low budget. Yet I have the cheek—the innocence?—to ask a newly elected Taoiseach to come on one, his very first programme on television too. My contact with him is Bertie O'Dowd, a man with the extraordinary record of having been private secretary to every taoiseach since the foundation of the state up to that, apart from the first, W. T. Cosgrave. I had known Bertie from my civil service days, had dealt with him whenever my old lord and master, Minister Seán MacEntee, was putting proposals for legislation before the government—a tough old station which, however, does me no harm at all in his eyes in what I am looking for now. But the Taoiseach is only a few weeks in office. Television interviews were not as common then as they are now, so it does not surprise me when Bertie tells me that I 'have a hell of a neck'. He will ask just the same. 'Tell him,' I say in a parting shot, 'that if he has any questions about me, to ring his brother, Finbarr.' Bertie comes back to me in a few minutes to say that the Taoiseach will be glad to do the show.

'Did he talk to Finbarr?' I ask.

'You're not supposed to ask and I'm not supposed to tell you. But put it this way. I don't think knowing Finbarr did you any harm.'

I think of the Irish 'sean-fhocal': 'Is fearr cara sa chúirt ná punt sa sparán.' I think also what a stroke of luck it is to be 'a neighbour's child'.

It is the first of many programmes I do with him. After that, whenever I ask him, if at all possible, he comes on and is always warmly welcomed, especially on some of the big 'Trom agus Éadrom' shows we do in Cork—including the first ever such show which was repeated on RTÉ following his funeral twenty-two years later; even more so, on the 'Up for the Final' Eve of All-Ireland shows, when his old hurling and football prowess comes into play. On the very last such programme he does with me, he asks to be put down in the front row with the other old hurlers and footballers who would be there; but when I tell him that, if I do that, I might as well scrap the panel altogether and spend the night down front with them, he goes along with what I propose. And after his friend, Séamus Murphy, the Cork sculptor, died, I do a commemorative programme on him on which Jack is to be the principal guest. He knew Séamus from away back when he passed his stoneyard in Blackpool on his way out to the Glen Rovers field on Dublin Hill. But on the night the programme is being made, he rings up to ask if he can be excused—he has a bad cold, has been up and down the country half a dozen times the previous week—in a word, he is exhausted. I say yes, of course we can manage, but it won't be the same without him. Then, faithfully, at eight o'clock, just as we are about to start, he turns up. In this, as on so many other occasions, he shows yet again the loyalty of 'a neighbour's child'.

That is 1976 and he is then three years out of power. In

May the following year I am at Writers' Week in Listowel when he arrives in town as part of his nationwide election tour. Anyone looking at the reception he gets will be in no doubt that there is a great groundswell building up in his favour. The whole town turns out. There are bands and banners everywhere. It is Harty Cup time all over again some forty-three years after that event in 1934. Only now it is happening, not for one school in one part of the city of Cork, but in every town and city in Ireland.

I was with him in RTÉ on the night of that famous 84 seat victory. John Hume wanted to have an urgent word with him and, in the midst of all the jubilation and turmoil, I was able to arrange that they meet in a quiet room in the Radio Centre. When it was over, some of us in the broadcasting world joined them for a drink. As we sat around chatting, Jack spotted a paper clip on the floor which, I couldn't help noticing, he picked up and put in his pocket. Well now, I think to myself, that's a bit strange—a national hero, the most popular man in Ireland, leader of the biggest party, about to become Taoiseach, and here he is picking up and putting in his pocket a single paper clip. He must have noticed the look of surprise on my face.

'A thing like that could come in very handy', he says.

A psychologist might trace it back to that childhood of his under Shandon, when to miss the chance of picking up so unusual a thing as a paper clip would have been considered a wanton waste. Incidentally—and in the light of events in more recent times—it may not be too flippant a comment to say that it was probably the only piece of public property that Jack Lynch ever appropriated!

Following his election as Taoiseach after that 1977 election, he appoints a number of new senators, one of whom is Dr T. K. Whitaker, former secretary of the

Department of Finance and Governor of the Central Bank. More relevant from my point of view is that he is Cathaoirleach of Bord na Gaeilge. When he goes to the Senate the Gaeilge job falls vacant; but before going he puts my name to Denis Gallagher, the new Gaeltacht Minister, to replace him. With the plethora of jobs I am doing at that time—Assistant Programme Controller in RTÉ, the weekly 'Trom agus Éadrom' and the daily radio 'Slán Abhaile', my hands are full. Denis, patient man that he is, has to ask me three times before I finally agree. He later tells me that the reason he persisted was that Jack Lynch was keen on it, though, he says, he was also keen that I stay in the running for advancement in the hierarchy of RTÉ. Effectively, however, it put paid to any ambitions I had in that direction. Maybe that was as well. RTÉ had in its time driven me to distraction; if I had gone higher there, I would probably have returned the compliment and driven it to distraction as well. There are some poisoned cups which are surely better left untasted!

This is a personal memoir and these are personal asides from the story of a major political life. Jack Lynch was, as we know, at the helm twice during the Sixties and Seventies, a turbulent time in the life of Ireland. Once in that time—it was the night of the sacking of Charles Haughey and Neil Blaney—I was with his brother Finbarr in his home near Cobh in Cork when I tell him that what had happened had greatly surprised me. Quite genuinely, I say I did not think Jack had the gumption to make such a drastic decision—he was far too nice and gentle a man. Brothers know each other better than anyone else and Finbarr's response was a shaft of insight.

'That's a mistake people who don't know Jack are likely to make,' he tells me. 'But what he has is enormous *negative* strength. If there is some direction he does not want to go, nothing on earth will make him take it. That's the Jack Lynch people are seeing today.'

The Arms Crisis which caused those sackings and what subsequently happened are but one part of the story of Jack Lynch's place in the shaping of modern Ireland. That is not the story here. The historians and political pundits will write the books on that. Nevertheless, seeing things from my sideline point of view, perhaps there are a few things I may say.

The first of these relates to Northern Ireland. The recurringly explosive situation there during his years in office could easily have led to a Bosnian/Kosovo crisis here, had his ability to calm things and keep the dogs of war at bay not prevailed. His much-repeated line that the situation must be dealt with peacefully, with a view to bringing reconciliation and agreement, surely laid the groundwork for the later peaceful overtures that have now begun to bear fruit.

His 'we shall not stand by' speech, delivered in the wake of Bloody Sunday, had some wildcat elements within his own ranks demanding immediate and aggressive retribution, pressures which only a man of 'enormous negative strength' could have withstood. To succumb to them at that time would certainly have created armed confrontation, from which there would be little prospect of escape without massive and recurrent bloodshed. As we know now, there was enough fire-power about for that to happen; once the two sovereign governments got involved—and with the mindset of some of the hawk-like Tories in Westminster, to say nothing of the later Falklands mindset of Lady Macbeth Thatcher—that was by no means a far-fetched possibility.

Half a century after the foundation of the state following the War of Independence, the idea of a new Anglo-Irish War was a prospect too terrible to contemplate. It was the personal calm of Jack Lynch and his deep commitment to a peaceful settlement that saved a whole generation of Irish people from that.

Secondly, though it did not happen without strife, such was the strength of his own charisma that he was able to hold his party together, more or less united, through it all. True, there were defections, the Blaney/Boland one being the worst; but there was no major exodus such as happened later, and certainly none that would affect the electoral majority he won in 1969 and the landslide majority he won in 1977. That was another achievement of consequence, both for his party and for the nation as a whole. For at that time, faced with the brazen intransigence of successive Tory governments in Westminster, the existence of strong, united leadership on this side of the water was essential to a firm negotiatory stance.

Finally, there was the landmark of Ireland's accession to the European Union achieved under his leadership, of which we have been major beneficiaries since. It is indeed a fact that there was no major opposition to this at the time—those who did oppose it have gone remarkably silent since. Nevertheless, it must stand to his credit that it was under his guidance that the dream of Wolfe Tone, the Fenians and the men of 1916—including fellow Corkman Michael Collins whom he admired so much—was finally realised: 'to break the connection with England' and launch us, with an independent voice, into a new form of union; one where, in Robert Emmet's phrase, Ireland would proudly 'take her place among the nations of the earth'.

All that is, as I say, for the political commentators and the history books. What I am about here are some personal links with a man I first saw with a hurling team when I was 5 years old and last saw sixty-odd years later when the sound and fury of all the intervening years was over. When the tenement house at No. 2 Blarney Street where I was born was demolished and a new terrace of townhouses put up in its place, Jack Lynch came down to open it. Thoughtfully, Cork City Manager Joe McHugh invited me along to be there too. As we stood out front beside what had once been the 'Green Garden' where I had played as a child—and where his brother Finbarr with his pals would come whistling out my big brother Ken to join them—the sound of the bells of Shandon came tumbling out over the Northside roofs.

Ken is long since dead; most of the lads whistling him out on those nights long ago are dead too. Jack Lynch is now with them. If, as we are told, 'in my Father's house there are many rooms', there is surely one for them. But, however grand those rooms may be, they will not be home unless they have the bells of Shandon ringing out the quarter-hours for them through all eternity.

Red Hats and Red Faces
CARDINAL TOMÁS Ó FIAICH

I don't know when I first heard the name Tomás Ó Fiaich. I must have been aware of it before a certain night in the early Sixties when he came on to a television programme about a report by the Commission on the Irish Language. This report was the result of several years' work by the commission, of which he was chairman, voluminous in length, breadth and depth—so much so that poor Tomás would later say that he had wasted seven years of his life on it. It was not the first or the last time that seven years of a good man's life were wasted on something that seemed to have more to do with pretence, make-believe and window-dressing than with any real and positive advance. The Latin poet Horace puts it well: 'Parturient montes et nascitur ridiculus mus' (The mountains are in labour and a ridiculous mouse is born).

On that particular night, Tomás was getting a hard time of it when Liam Mac Gabhann, a kindly soul who knew the man he had, comes to his aid by addressing him as 'Father Tom'. Immediately he hears it—it is how he is known by his own people in south Armagh—he is at ease; and goes on to make as convincing a case for the language as I have ever heard. From that night on, so far as I am concerned, he will be the best-tempered, best-informed, best-liked apologist the language has.

It so happens that his commission's report will shortly turn up in my own life. This is when it becomes my job as a civil service executive to collect the views and responses of the Department of Health on its recommendations. The views and responses are not good. In effect, what they say is that to try to implement the ideas in the report in any realistic way will bring the health services to a halt. When this sanguine message is finally ready to be sent off to the Department of Finance which is running the show, I take it upon myself to put up with it a draft letter from Minister Seán MacEntee to Finance Minister Dr Jim Ryan, both old 1916 men and comrades-in-arms of the Irish language visionaries of the Easter Rising. More to the point, both are close collaborators with Taoiseach de Valera, whose brain child this commission was.

The letter, buried now somewhere in the vaults of Upper Merrion Street, is short and sweet and makes but one salient point: having summarised the Department's uniformly negative response, it goes on to state the seminal role the language played in the reawakening of the national spirit, out of which a goodly part of the whole impetus for independence had come. Now that the new nation is up and running, it goes on, is it honourable to the men who launched it to jettison what they had set their hearts on in the first place? Hence, for anything like a positive response to this commission's recommendations to be achieved, a new approach was going to be needed to re-educate the public in the role of the language in the formation of a mature, self-confident national identity.

MacEntee signs the letter and off it goes. Subsequently, when the finance people produce their White Paper outlining the measures to be taken to implement the recommendations, there is this long and acrimonious debate on the whole restoration issue; and in the course of this Seán Lemass, by then Taoiseach, uses that same argument, even down to the very phrase, 're-educate the public in the role of the language', which that letter contained.

So from the mid-sixties on, Tomás Ó Fiaich's name will be constantly to the fore whenever the language is being discussed. He is the leading light in Cumann na Sagart, originally based in Maynooth but soon to spread nationwide; in due course they launch the successful 'Glór na Gael' annual competition—a kind of 'Tidy Towns' for the language. Maynooth, in its 200-year-old history, has not been a notable language champion; nor, with notable exceptions, has the Catholic hierarchy ever gone much out of its way to help it. On the contrary, again with notable exceptions such as Archbishop John McHale of Tuam, there were important voices within the Catholic establishment ever since Daniel O'Connell, who felt that it was a backward-looking, retrogressive influence, keeping the populace poor, isolated and out of touch with the great movements of the Catholic world. Despite this, Glór na Gael and Cumann na Sagart do manage to build up a significant national following, with a whole new fund of goodwill to back it up. Tomás is central to all this. Inevitably, it carries the risk of public controversy, of which the hierarchy, ever since the days of the Fenians and Parnell, is in mortal dread.

It becomes a reality when he is one of four apologists for the language at a wild and potentially riotous forum in the Mansion House one night, under the sponsorship of the anti-compulsory Irish Language Freedom Movement, the LFM. The night ends in uproar and the following day there are the predictable scandal-mongering headlines. Despite his good standing as professor of history in Maynooth and his well-known friendship with Cardinal Conway whose protégé he is, it is widely thought that this has put paid to his chances of ever becoming what many thought he would become—an independent and strongly national-minded Irish bishop. 'The LFM', one headline had it, 'knocks mitre off Ó Fiaich's head.'

For a time it looks indeed as if that might be true. But he is still a scholar and that they cannot take from him. His historical research, meticulous, exhaustive and, for the most part, carried out entirely by himself, is nowhere shown to better effect than in his fine book, *Gaelscrínte i gCéin* (Irish Shrines Abroad). In this he follows the footsteps of the Irish monks from the sixth century on. Years later, when the 'Radharc' team under Father Dermod McCarthy does a television series with him, I learn that all the splendid scholarly research—from places as far apart as Iona, Lindisfarne, Cologne, Würtzberg, Trier, Liège, Auxerre, Luxeuil, Vienna and Salzburg—was the result of his summer holidays, for years spent walking over the ground where those monks had walked centuries before him.

I get a first-hand example of the quality of this research one night when I go to visit him in Maynooth during his time as professor of history there. The section in James Joyce's story 'The Dead' in *Dubliners* has a Miss Ivors upbraiding Gabriel Conroy for going to France or Germany on his holidays—'to keep in touch with the language'.

'Haven't you your own language to keep in touch with— Irish?' she asks. 'Haven't you your own land to visit . . . that you know nothing of, your own people and your own country?'

When he fails to answer her, she walks away from him, whispering in his ear the traitorous phrase, 'West Briton'. Tomás tracked down the date of writing of 'The Dead', then the minutes of the meetings of the Keating Branch of the

Dublin Gaelic League where the young James Joyce had some friends. There he found a Miss Sheehy, an ardent cultural nationalist, campaigning vigorously for Irish people to spend their holidays in the Gaeltachts in Ireland as a means of improving their fluency in the language. She became the model for Miss Ivors in 'The Dead'. But it is not her sole claim to fame: the same lady would in due course marry a young Dublin journalist, a marriage which in time would produce a son—one Conor Cruise O'Brien.

Anyone who knew Ó Fiaich knew this historian's passion for research. Even the most casual meeting would stimulate it. He would quiz somebody he had just met about his name and where he came from—not just county or town, but district, parish, street—and then bring up all sorts of interesting associations with it. In this, in the very best sense, he shows the traits of the ancient Irish 'seanchaí', someone who told you, not just the story and the characters in the story, but facts and details about their people before them. This might seem to some like the typical Irish village gossip; but in his case, all that intimate detail is sifted and fitted together to remake a whole picture of a once integrated, but for centuries fissurated, past.

It will come out most markedly when he is among his own people in Cullyhanna and Crossmaglen. His knowledge of the literary traditions of that area is encyclopaedic; which is the reason I invite him to be consultant and guide for a television programme we are making in the region of Urney and Forkhill in south Armagh for the first ever 'Éigse Peadar Ó Doirnín', an eighteenth-century Ulster poet. The programme 'Féach' has Peter Kennerly as director, Áine O'Connor as production assistant and Breandán Ó hEithir as reporter and front man (all three of them, with Tomás, now dead—beannacht dílis Dé leo go léir). I get Albert Fry down from Belfast to sing Ó Doirnín's 'aisling' poem 'Úr-Chnoc Chéin Mhic Cáinte', which he does most poignantly at the memorial stone over the poet's burial place in Urney graveyard, with Slieve Gullion in the background, the Gap of the North not far away. All goes well until Kennerly decides that the song needs a bit more than Albert Fry sitting on a headstone strumming his guitar. Breandán has given him a quick run-down on the story line: the beautiful maiden of the 'aisling' appears to the poet in his reverie and recites the wrongs and hopes of Mother Ireland. As luck—or ill-luck— would have it, the mini-skirt is very much the fashion at the time and Áine, certainly among the most beautiful young women in Ireland then or ever, is wearing one to perfection. So Kennerly puts the idea to Breandán that in a few cut-away shots we will see her striding through the lush grass— the 'spéir-bhean' on her way to the enraptured, day-dreaming poet.

Breandán, politic as always, but knowing Kennerly's eye for beauty—the beauty of women not excluded—judges that, though the idea sounds good, it will be wise to seek the view of the editor and consultant (i.e. Tomás and me). Celibate cleric and long-married spouse though we are, we cannot fail to be impressed by the picture our visually sensitive film director proposes to us: that of an 'aisling-woman' coming towards the poet who, if he is at all sensible, will surely remain happily drowsed for the rest of his life!

It all happens as planned. We go back to RTÉ, where the film is edited, to be shown the following Sunday, the final day of the 'Éigse' weekend. A lengthy convoy of cars follows our leader, Tomás Ó Fiaich, as he leads us through the Ó Doirnín country of Forkhill and Crossmaglen. There is a divine miscontrivance in these things: at the precise time the programme goes on air, we have arrived at the house of the local parish priest, one Canon Mac Íomhair, where we are invited to come in and see it going out live, which we duly do. We see Albert Fry at the headstone, his singing dulcet and clear as always; we hear Breandán tell the story of Ó Doirnín and the poets with their 'aislingí'; and then we see Áine's turbulent thighs bestriding the lush grasses of the Cúchulain fable-land. It is without doubt a most spectacular sight—David Lean (*Dr Zhivago, Ryan's Daughter*) would have given his eye teeth for it; as would any young male student who, if he had the good fortune to have 'Úr-Chnoc Chéin Mhic Cáinte' on his course that year, would have it printed on his memory for the rest of his life.

Our host, Canon Mac Íomhair, sits there in silence, our priest-consultant historian beside him. Then we get up to go.

'Cad ba dhóigh leat dó'? Tomás enquires.

The Canon, wise man that he is, and a lover of the language too, takes his time about answering. When he does, it is to say what we all know: that it is indeed a distinguished piece of film work and that all concerned are to be congratulated. Then, after a further pause, he adds a perceptive rider: 'Dá mba í sin an spéirbhean a bhí á feiscint ag Ó Doirnín, ní thógfá ar an bhfear bocht é dá bhfanfadh sé ina chodladh go deo.' (If that's the vision-woman Ó Doirnín was looking at, you wouldn't blame the poor man for staying asleep for good!).

There would be more serious themes and times. Later, when I am planning a television series on the situation in Northern Ireland, Tomás comes very much into the picture. My idea with this series is to attempt to explain the two cultures to each other in a mutually sympathetic way. What is their background? What are the root causes of their conflict?

Can they be persuaded to have some sort of understanding for each other when this is intelligently explained? And, out of that, is there a possibility of some common ground on which they can come together in peace and amity?

My first thoughts on the series—provisionally entitled 'The Red Hand'—are rudimentary; but from such knowledge as I have of things up north, I believe I may have had the core of the idea from the start. I have some insights from the writings of people like Forrest Reid, Sam Thompson, John Boyd, St John Ervine and Sam Hanna Bell, and from the ballad and music work of David Hammond, the MacPeakes, Tommy Makem, Tony McAuley and Bill Meek. I also have some knowledge of the Irish language and poetry side, though nothing like enough for what I am about to attempt now. So before any real progress can be made, I am going to need someone—on the lines of the consulting editors for the Thomas Davis lectures on radio—probably a historian, to advise me. This is where Tomás Ó Fiaich comes in. I send him an outline of my thinking, with the broad dimensions of what we are likely to end up with: a season of half-hour programmes, with a summary programme at the end to review what was said and maybe point to possible future directions.

His rooms in Maynooth, where I regularly visit him to discuss the idea after that, are truly a scholar's den, with books, papers and journals scattered all over the place (incidentally, no different, when he got there, from his rooms in Armagh, where the scholar and the historian took pride of place over the churchman and cardinal)! Like all people with a passion for their subject, he knows exactly where things are and, at a moment's notice, can put his hand on whatever fact or nugget of information he needs. Occasionally I am brought to lunch in the staff common room, where the prevailing convention is that, if there is a guest present, they may have wine; which is surely the reason why I am accorded a heartier welcome than I feel I deserve.

In due course, Tomás formulates a set of titles on which the programmes will be based. I have them here before me as I write:

(1)   *The Gap of the North*: Ulster of the legends, Cúchulain, Táin Bó Cuailgne in Tom Kinsella's translation, the Déirdre story, the Children of Lir; visual remains: Giant's Causeway, Eamhain Macha.

(2)   *Saints and Scholars*: Patrick , Colmcille, Brigid; Armagh, Derry, Bangor, Moville; Patrick, the shepherd boy on Slemish, Doire, Iona, Book of Armagh, Patrick's Breastplate.

(3)   *My Fathers Followed Theirs*: The O'Neills, O'Donnells, Maguires; the MacDonnells of Antrim; Col. Owen Roe in the Netherlands; Shane O'Neill in Elizabeth's Court; Louvain, Salamanca, Rome.

(4)   *The Proud Planters*: 1609, 1641, Cromwell; the Hamiltons, Chichesters, Brookes; contemporary maps, Chart's book on the Derry Plantation.

(5)   *The Underground Nation*: Peadar Ó Doirnín, Dall Mac Cuarta, Art Mac Cubhthaigh; the Mass-houses, Penal Crosses, Patterns; Protestant Irish language lovers, e.g. MacAdam.

(6)   *The Planters' First Stand*: Derry, Enniskillen, the Boyne; the 12 July Parades, Linen-halls, new town with square or diamond.

(7)   *The Common Name of Irishman*: Tone, Russell, Henry Joy McCracken, Jemmy Hope, the Reverend Porter; independent-minded Presbyterians: Peep o' Day Boys, Defenders; Cave Hill where 'the common name of Irishman' began.

(8)   *Industrial Giant*: The foundation of Belfast, shipyards, linen mills; sectarian riots begin; the bleaching-greens; the rise of the working class and the ghetto mentality.

(9)   *Divide and Rule*: The Union, Lord Castlereagh, Orange Societies, Ribbonmen, the Mollies; Ulster Fenians, including Protestants; 'Ulster will fight and Ulster will be right.'

(10)   *Divided We Stand*: The story since 1921.

(11)   *Placenames, Family Names*: Eamhain Macha, Downpatrick, Derry, Dunseverick, Aileach, Armagh, Falls Road, Shankill Road; the Protestant national cultural tradition.

(12)   *Literature, Music, Song, Dance*: Carleton, Ferguson, Sam Hanna Bell; Brendan Adams and the Ulster Folk Museum; 'The Sash', 'Lillibulero', 'Úir-Chill an Chreagáin', 'Úr-Chnoc Chéin Mhic Cáinte'; Mulholland Traditional Dancers in Belfast; Louis MacNeice, W. R. Rodgers, John Montague, Brian Friel, Seamus Heaney.

(13)   *Look Back in Hope*: Résumé and Open Forum.

Reading back over it now after all the years, it still strikes me as a very good beginning. RTÉ was keen enough on the idea, as was Ronnie Mason, then BBC controller in Belfast, who saw it as fruitful ground for co-production. We even got to the point of commissioning a pilot script, lost somewhere now in the bowels of RTÉ. Tomás had suggested that this be done by his old Armagh friend, a most knowledgeable but modest man, Seán Ó Baoill. It was about the Belfast Harp Festival of 1796 and the then largely Protestant Gaelic Society. With his impish sense of humour, Seán entitled it 'Strum, Strum And Bedamned!' If ever it got to air, it would surely have struck an intimate chord with both communities who, whatever their other faults and failings, would have taken kindly to some of its music and songs. But, alas, it was not to be.

All that is a long time ago. In more recent times, I get an idea of how the series might have looked from my 'Lifelines' programme with David Ervine of the Northern Progressive Unionist Party. This turns out to be a great night's 'craic' and celebration, the two cultures getting an equal airing, with a moving rendition of 'The Quiet Land of Erin' (from the Irish 'Aird Tí Chuain') by Davy's brother; a Lambeg drum, the racket from which nearly drives us all raving mad out of Studio 1; and Davy's own response when I tell him that his is the oldest Irish name in the place that night (from 'Éireamhoin', one of the three sons of Milesius, the first Celtic invaders).

'I'm glad to hear it's older than yours anyway, Billy Murphy!'

Solas na bhFlaitheas dó. Tomás is well gone by then and our joint brain child never sees the light of day. Shortly after his outline was written, Bloody Sunday happens, and the whole enterprise falls through. Whatever else might be considered for television from then on, a series aimed at promoting amity and understanding between the two cultures was not! By the time it was—and only now at the beginning of this new millennium does it seem at all possible—both I and, more importantly, Tomás had long since moved on. His public life we know about from then on—as President of Maynooth, as Archbishop of Armagh, then as Cardinal. But I am certain that his instinct for the success of that series, if it ever got to be made, was well founded. Maybe in some heaven where he surely is, along with those saints and scholars of old that he knew so well, maybe something like it can happen; but in the melting pot that the North of Ireland had been for many years after his time, it would take nothing short of an Irish miracle for it to happen there!

On a number of occasions after that he will be a most welcome guest on my television shows. His first public appearance as Cardinal coincides with the All-Ireland football final between Armagh and Dublin. That very week he was in Rome where, he tells us in advance, he may be delayed. So we are to make contingency plans in case he cannot be there. But his beloved Armagh being involved, he will not miss that 'Up for the Final' Eve of All-Ireland celebration for love or money. Wild horses, not to mind lesser things like popes and cardinals, will not keep him away. He arrives in Dublin Airport late and comes straight to the studio, where a tumultuous welcome awaits him, led naturally by his own 'Boys of the County Armagh'. Listening to that applause and, more stupendously, to their roar in Croke Park the following day when Jimmy Smith leads them on to the field, one might be forgiven for thinking that no team on earth, let alone the petty Dubs of 'Heffo's army', will stop them.

But the game has hardly started when Jimmy Keaveney of Dublin, going for a point, spots a gap as wide as a gate in the Armagh goalmouth and shoots for goal. That early score sends shock waves through Armagh from which they never recover. And later that night a somewhat chastened Tomás, guest of honour at their celebration dinner, takes refuge in the old Irish sean-fhocal, 'Beidh lá eile ag an bPaorach'. Faraor, a Thomáis, a chroí—go dtí an lá inniu féin, ní raibh!

So, after all the years, first as a student, then a scholar, then a professor, then a registrar and finally as president, at last he leaves Maynooth and takes up residence in Ara Coeli as Archbishop of Armagh. The Maynooth ambience, originally based on the great Catholic universities of Europe—Paris, Louvain, Bordeaux, Rome—is one of scholarly fellowship and high cordiality with, inevitably, occasional internal combustions between men of character and commitment; women have not yet seriously entered the scene but soon will, with predictable consequences for some, including some of Tomás's close friends. I remember nights in their company there when the conversation develops like some Renaissance dialectic—our own home-grown Aquinases, Abelards and Duns Scotuses, probing and dissecting the known and unknown world into the small hours!

And then suddenly it all stops. Cardinal Conway dies; it is widely thought that he will be replaced by one of the existing bishops—Philbin of Belfast is mentioned, as is Cahal Daly of Longford—but to the surprise of many, not least that dismal hack who had 'knocked the mitre' off Tomás's head during the LFM row long before, the name that comes out is Tomás Ó Fiaich. Church politics being notably secretive, few will ever know the full story of how that came about. My own guess, for what it is worth, is that the democratisation brought about by the Second Vatican Council had given some priority to the voice of diocesan clergy when it came to the selection of their bishop; and even though Tomás was away from his native place for several years by then, anyone who had ever seen him in the company of his fellow priests up there would be in no doubt, once given the choice, as to who their choice would be. So off up north he goes to wear his cardinal's red hat.

What lay folk like me will best remember about that day is the great party afterwards, with the Irish language and culture much to the fore. And why should it not be? He is the first Armagh man to hold that office since the reformer, Malachi, in the twelfth century!

Nobody ever ran as diverse and multicultural a party as Tomás did. But the murder and mayhem up north are well under way by now and most of the guests leave early to be home before dark. Whether from the old habit of the Maynooth days or some more elemental Celtic strain in us, a few of us southerners are among the last to leave. As we drive away, there he is standing at the door waving to us, the red cincture about his ample girth and the pipe, as always, clenched in his teeth. Behind him in the lighted hallway stands the Ara Coeli housekeeper, Sister Malachi, a lovely lady by all means, but well on in years. Instead of the boisterous and scholarly jousting within the hallowed halls of Maynooth, this will be the company about him from now on. It is surely one of the loneliest sights I have ever seen.

Driving down through south Armagh and on into Louth that night, the conversation turns to some contemporary scandal in the realm of sexual affairs, something that was in the headlines at the time and the subject of current debate—unusual enough then, certainly not the flood-tide of such events since. Whatever it was, it reminds one of the company, a classicist, of other sexual aberrations in the Greek and Roman world long ago.

I add my own ha'porth to this—gleaned during my schooldays in Cork's North Mon.—about the begetting of one Scipio Africanus, an extremely astute and cunning man, the prototype of all devious and conniving politicians since! The classical historian Livy attributes his serpentine cunning to the fact that, at his conception, his mother's handmaidens actually saw a serpent slide out through the window of her boudoir after he has planted his serpent seed! From this, the conversation easily progresses to the women of Lesbos who sought satisfaction with their own kind after their menfolk have all gone off to war; and, later, to other deviations—as with Scipio, not always with humans—where bewildered quadrupeds, willing or unwilling, were pressed into urgent service by the lord of the beasts! These stories are told to us by the classicist, first in Greek, then in Latin, then in English for those who cannot understand. And after each solemn recounting of these dread events, there follows the sapient footnote: 'There you are, my children. Nothing new under the sun!'

I cannot say what Tomás might have thought of this conversation among his friends; as a canny churchman, he would no doubt have been obliged to disapprove. But, in his own oft-repeated phrase, '*sub specie aeternitatis*', he would also be obliged to accept that, in the recurrent processes of a sometimes strange and twisted life, there is indeed, as the man said, 'nothing new under the sun'.

One of Tomás's most revealing contributions to early Irish missionary history is that it had little or nothing of the character of modern foreign missionary movements at all. The motive uppermost in the minds of the *peregrini* was that of personal mortification and self-sacrifice—to renounce home and family and seek out some secluded spot where the ties of the world would not interfere with the pursuit of sanctity. Colmcille's voyage to Iona in A.D. 563 was not primarily a missionary journey at all, though it would become that as time went on. In the meantime, he was the prototype for later generations of the patriotic exile, thinking longingly in a foreign land of the little places at home which he loved so much. This is the 'white martyrdom' of the people in his fine book, *Gaelscrínte i gCéin*—Colmcille,

Columbanus, Fiacre, Fursey, Cillian—men who left home and country and the people they loved to travel often perilous roads, occasionally following the trading caravans into the far corners of the then known world, where they discovered a whole universe which knew nothing about religion and had never heard the name of Christ.

While the merchants' stalls sold grain and stock and worldly goods, they put up signs saying that what they had for sale were the virtues of love and wisdom and understanding. And the princes and potentates, at first menacing, then curious, then stimulated, and finally captivated by this strange but eloquent message, took to the new idea and became Christianised.

In a *tour de force* talk he gave under the auspices of Gael Linn some time before his death, he went over the ground those saintly journeymen had walked—from Iona and Lindisfarne to Auxerre, Luxeuil, Würtzburg, Vienna, St Gall, Bobbio, even as far east as Kiev—all responding to that strange call recorded in the earliest sermon which has survived in the native language from that time: 'Is í an bánmartra do dhuine, an tan scaras, ar son Dé, re gach rud a charas.' (White martyrdom for a person is when he leaves everything he loves for the sake of God.) In his contribution to the 'Course of Irish History' TV series, Tomás cites the example of the greatest of them.

'Colmcille inspired his namesake, Columbanus, to go further afield a generation later; and England, France, Belgium, Germany, Switzerland, Austria and Italy would soon re-echo to the tramp of Irish monks. Luxeuil, the greatest of Columbanus's foundations in France, was destined to influence nearly one hundred other houses before the year 700. His journey from Luxeuil to Italy, like another Patrick or another Paul, was surely one of the great missionary voyages of history—twice across France, up the Rhine to Switzerland, across Lake Constance to Bregenz in Austria, southward through the Alps and northern Italy till he founded his last monastery at Bobbio in the year 613.'

Tomás Ó Fiaich had been to all those places himself and knew them well. That was one clear indication that, in his time, he was the man uniquely suited to be head of the widespread Irish Catholic Church.

My last association with him will be a self-portrait documentary for the series, 'Mo Scéal Féin', which we shot in Armagh; in his birthplace, Cullyhanna, near Crossmaglen; and in Maynooth where he had spent twenty-eight years of his working life. Looking at it now, it is hard to believe that he had only a short time to live: there he is cycling through the streets of Armagh, a sprightly, smiling figure in shirt sleeves; later, in a field in front of his parents' house in Cullyhanna where he talks about them; later again, with the O'Neills of ancient history—'Géaga ghlan-daite Néill fhrasaigh is Gaeil Thír Eoghain'—in the old Creggan cemetery 'Úir-Chill an Chreagáin'. It so happens that a film crew from Bayerischer Rundfunk in Munich are making a programme about him at the same time; and in the lengthy interview he does with them, he speaks perfectly fluent German; St Killian of Würtzburg, who hailed from the nearby village of Mullagh in Cavan—one of that 'white martyrdom' brigade—would have been proud! Towards the end of our programme, he is standing on the steps of St Patrick's, looking out over the roofs and gables of the 'Cathedral city' towards the square tower of the Church of Ireland St Patrick's half a mile away.

'It will not happen in my lifetime,' he says, 'but I look

forward to a time when there will be only one St Patrick's here, serving all the people equally.'

And then suddenly, with no hint or warning, Tomás Ó Fiaich is dead. He had indeed been recovering from the flu and had a bad cough when he led the Armagh diocesan pilgrimage to Lourdes, which he probably shouldn't have done. But, with his unsuppressible good humour and natural ebullience, no one thought for a minute that, in his case, the flu or a cough could be life threatening.

Like all such events, the time and place when I hear the news—it's at a party celebrating the opening of a new hotel in Dalkey—will be printed for ever on my memory.

'Isn't that terrible news about the Cardinal?'

'What news?'

'He's dead. It was on RTÉ just now. He died in Lourdes earlier today.'

Tomás dead! Tomás Ó Fiaich! Dear, dear 'sagart a rún'— 'Father Tom!' All that rich celebration of Irish life, all that hearty laughter, all that restless, searching mind and soul, all that light and life gone out for good! Upon how slim a thread we are suspended between life and death!

The following morning, I am with the family on the flight to Lourdes to bring him back. When we arrive, there he is in the airport mortuary chapel, laid out in his canonical robes. But it is not the Tomás we knew. He is too uncannily quiet. Which language, I ask myself, did he speak to the doctors and nurses who attended him at the end? Like that great favourite of his, Columbanus of Luxeuil and Bobbio, it could have been any of half a dozen. As the coffin is brought out into the morning air, the sun comes up over the foothills of the Pyrenees, throwing long shadows over the tarmac. And as

the flight circles out over Lourdes and sets its course
northward into the skies, it will pass over the territories
where Columbanus walked close on fourteen centuries
before. For Tomás, unlike him, it was not to be 'white
martyrdom', exiled for ever from the place he loved. For he is
on his way back, back to Armagh, a kindly judgment upon
the chronicler of all that generation of *peregrini pro nomine
Christi*; from the very first of them, Colmcille of Derry who,
like Tomás himself, never wavered in the love for his native
place:

> Ionmhain Durmhagh is Doire,
> Ionmhain Rath-Bhoth go nglaine
> Ionmhain Druim Thuama is mín meas,
> Ionmhain Sórd is Ceanannas.

> Dá mba liom Alba uile
> Otha a broinne go a bile,
> Dob fhearr liomsa áit toighe
> Agam ar lár caomh-Dhoire.

> My heart's love Durrow, Derry,
> Raphoe, my love be with thee,
> Drumtomey, gentle, unsurpassed,
> Swords and Kells, my sweetness.

> If all of Scotland were my own,
> Its every tree and stick and stone,
> I still would choose for my abode
> Dear gentle-hearted Derry.

From West Bank to West Cork

SEÁN Ó RIADA

I am on my way on the suburban line from Dún Laoghaire into my office in the Custom House. The platform at Dún Laoghaire is crowded, as is the train when it comes in. It is the non–stop which arrives in Tara Street at 9 a.m. The year is 1961.

I go to the nearest door that opens before me and step in. 'Good morning, Liam', someone in there greets me. It is Thomas Kinsella, poet, critic and—closer to my life at the time—civil servant in the Department of Finance. He has someone beside him who moves up to make a place for me.

'This is a friend,' he says, 'Seán Ó Riada . . . Liam Ó Murchú.'

A tall thin man with a goatee and reddish hair looks up from *The Irish Times* he is reading. He looks strange, a bit foreign, not your average suburban commuter.

'That's not Liam Ó Murchú, Tom,' he says. 'That's Bill Murphy.'

It is then my turn to correct. 'And that's not Seán Ó Riada, Tom. That's John Reidy.'

We are both right—and wrong. But how could Tom Kinsella possibly know? He would have to go back to a time when Bill Murphy was briefly in UCC, malingering on a scholarship with what passed for a study of the arts, but in reality marking time until he could abandon his all to the unlovely arms of civil servitude; and John Reidy was a student in the music department of that illustrious hall of learning, whiling away the night-hours playing jazz and boogie-woogie for the penniless, sweaty hopefuls during the weekend 'hops' in the Rest. For this he would earn the handsome sum of a shilling, maybe two if the crowd was good; if not, he might sing for his supper. But the prospects were promising: with luck and a few contacts, he might end up doing piano stand-ins for one of the big bands, with smoke-filled nights in the Gresham Rooms—who knows, even the star-studded Arcadia with a thousand and one even sweatier hopefuls by the banks of his own lovely Lee! And one day—dare he even dream of it?—he might get as far as the dope and sleaze of New Orleans. He might even reach the hallowed heights of Hollywood—our local boy, John Reidy, up there with the best of them: Louis 'Satchmo' Armstrong, Dizzy Gillespie, Hoagy Carmichael, even Jimmy 'Schnozzle' Durante who had worked his way to the top a long time ago, as he sang in his croaky crow-voice:

> It's Toscanini, Iturbi and me,
> We definitely are the big three.

I cannot believe that it was a future John's discerning, hard-working parents would have approved; even less so the dedicated and disciplined head of his department, Germanic son of a Germanic father, Professor Aloys Fleischmann. Nor was the jazz and boogie-woogie playing his sole talent: another was the game of push-penny, played in the table tennis room of the Rest. Here, with a coterie of other aficionados, he would prove himself equally adept with them—and equally penurious—until a lucky strike came. It was not the first or the last time that an artist would have starved in his garret but for the application of some highly inartistic skills. I do not have the impression that 'art' was a word much in John Reidy's vocabulary at that time; but, as many a good artist before and since knows, needs must when the devil drives, and a shilling lunch with a packet of fags to finish it off was a worthy recompense for whatever arts he might have practised on such trivial pursuits.

That morning on the train from Dún Laoghaire, I learn that he had recently spent some time in Paris where, with his wife, Ruth Coughlan, he was living it up on the Left Bank, habitat of writers and artists down through the years— Toulouse Lautrec, Picasso, Scott Fitzgerald, Hemingway and James Joyce. The cafés and bistros there would have given a ready welcome to a talented and personable young piano player who could adapt his skills to a variety of tastes. That side of Seán would have come as no surprise to anyone who had known him in the jazz and boogie-woogie years. What would come as a surprise would be his taking what in effect was a civil service job when he returned to Ireland—as assistant director of music in the old Radio Éireann. His lord and master there, Director of Music Gerard Victory, was in an equally ambivalent situation: a bright boy in school, he had been groomed for stardom in the 'legit' civil service, first the Department of Foreign Affairs, then Finance, then finally— surely a perverse piece of bureaucratic misassignment—in the Central Statistics Office. There, as I personally know, having worked with him, bulky and dog-eared files on the Cost of Living Index and Wholesale Prices Index Figure would sometimes land on our desks with stray pages sticking out of them covered with what looked suspiciously like musical scores. Gerry finally made his break for freedom by getting into the Radio Éireann Repertory Company and thence to its music department, while his assistant, Seán, probably still drowsed with the fumes of poppies from the Parisian Left Bank, fled from his bureaucratic enslavement almost as fast as he got into it—only to take up an even more life-threatening one, as Director of Music in the Abbey Theatre. There, with his mane of reddish hair and trim goatee, he could be seen nightly down in the orchestra pit, conducting from his piano stool his illustrious ensemble with the fire and passion of a Mahler—all three of them!

It so happens that I was with him on his last night there; it was also the final night of a one-act play in Irish by our mutual friend, Richard Power. This was put on after the main play in English, a feat of strategic planning which ensured an impressive audience—the author, his family and, if lucky, a few friends who, out of old loyalty, might turn up. So, small as his royalties were, Seán's pay was probably even smaller.

Still, ever the gentleman, ever the lavish *grand seigneur*, he insists on having us over to Mooney's of College Street afterwards to celebrate/commiserate with him on his return to the ranks of the unemployed. That is when we first hear that he is leaving Dublin, selling up lock, stock and barrel and going off down to live in Ballyferriter in the west Kerry Gaeltacht. It seems a mad idea to me and Dick Power but there is no doubting the romantic thrust. This latter-day child of the Left Bank—later again, of the cloying, artsy-craftsy life of Dublin—was getting back to the roots to renew his creative and artistic spirit.

What had turned the jazz and boogie-woogie John Reidy into the soul-searching Seán Ó Riada he had now become? I do not pretend to know the answer to that question. I have the impression—was it from Seán himself I heard it?—that his mother, from Kilnamantra in the west Cork Gaeltacht, must have had some Irish and so when he and the family went to live in Ballyferriter and, later again in Cúil Aodha, they were in a sense going home. All I can say with certainty is that his coming to the Irish language, following his return from Paris, had one point in common with my own: back in Dublin, he and Ruth had sent their children to the all-Irish school in Monkstown, Scoil Lorcáin. There, under the influence of the marvellous kindergarten teacher, Bean Uí Chadhain (wife of writer and academic, Máirtín), Irish quickly became the language of the home.

Bean Uí Chadhain had the ability to make children from English-speaking homes comfortably bilingual within the space of six months, a headline in language teaching which would really make you wonder at all the fuss that is made about the difficulty of teaching Irish to the young. It is an experience that is replicated in the multitude of all-Irish schools which have sprung up all over the country since, though I doubt if many teachers will ever equal the compelling charm of Bean Uí Chadhain as she went about her work.

Seán's film music for *Mise Éire* and *Saoirse* then comes on the scene to an avalanche of praise. Through it he comes into close contact with such superb Irish speakers as Pádraic Ó Raghallaigh and Liam Budhlaeir, an experience which surely improved his fluency.

The Ó Riadas have this big rambling old house in Galloping Green in Dublin's Stillorgan, and frequently have groups of traditional musicians gathering in the basement, including the nucleus of the now famous Chieftains; those he brought together for the first time during his stint as Director of Music in the Abbey as a backing group for *The Honey Spike* by Bryan MacMahon. But none of this traditional music activity, the language-learning and the rejected security led any of us to expect what they were all leading up to—the magnificent, cathartic explosion of the first of those films, *Mise Éire*. This was produced by George Morrison from the archives—old newsreel, stills and newspaper cuttings—about the period from the setting up of Sinn Féin in 1906, through 1916, up to the landslide election of 1919. It was indeed highly evocative material, carefully chosen and brilliantly put together; but what really made it, what put it away beyond all other archive-based documentaries before and since, was Ó Riada's sublime musical score.

The timing was relevant: it came in the wake of one of the bleakest periods in modern Irish economic history. Shortly before, the First Programme for Economic Expansion had been launched, master-minded by that practical-minded visionary, Dr T. K. Whitaker, under the leadership of old 1916 men, Dr Jim Ryan, Minister for Finance, and newly elected Taoiseach, Seán Lemass. The previous year, 1957, had been a black one. The emigration figures were catastrophic: it wasn't only the unemployed who were leaving; many who had good jobs were leaving too. It seemed only a matter of time until everyone would be gone. Then, suddenly, there is this new positive statement of economic plans and aims and with it a confident prediction that better times are on the way. For that, there would be a need for new courage, a new task-directed patriotism. I don't know how much of all that was in Seán's mind when he was writing the musical score for *Mise Éire*; what is certain is that his music caught the mood and temper of the time and put fresh hopes and ambitions into us all. What Dvořák had done for Czechoslovakia, Chopin for Poland, Sibelius for Finland, Seán Ó Riada, with *Mise*

Éire, did for Ireland. It was a crucible of the nation's dreams, its griefs and joys, its martyrdom and sublimation, swelling to the concluding titanic rapture of 'Róisín Dubh'. There were hundreds of balladeers about, thousands of traditional musicians and groups; their music had been done before and would undoubtedly be done again. But this statement in music of the Irish dream, without a word being spoken, did for us what mere words could never do: it established a new awareness, a new sense of pride in our own place and our own people, and a new dedication to see that sense of pride brought to fulfilment. It was our 'Cry, the Beloved Country' and went straight to the heart. Those of us so inspired by it could not but be moved to a new sense of national self-esteem. We were the first educated generation of freedom; *Mise Éire* called us to a new sense of purpose to make that freedom worthwhile.

After that, it seemed to some at least that Seán took a backward step. True, there was a little symphonic work later on, pieces with ponderous titles like 'Nomos' and 'Hercules Dux Ferrariae', but they made no comparable popular impact. Critic Charles Acton and he had it out in fine style in a series of articles in *The Irish Times*, a battle royal for what they each separately thought was the heart and soul of Irish music. By turning his back on the great European tradition and composers, Charles said, Seán was rejecting the huge classical future that *Mise Éire* had promised; Seán, for his part, said that there was no future in that past. His new inspiration came from the ancient Irish harp tradition, the music of O'Carolan and Ruairí Dall Ó Cathain, and, further afield, from the music of the Orient, India and China especially.

So, as the classical and symphonic side receded, the

traditional and folk side progressed. 'Reacaireacht an Riadaigh' and 'Fleá Cheoil an Radio' were highly popular radio programmes which did much to add prestige and standing to the traditional mode. The old airs and songs in Irish were given new and attractive settings, often led by Seán himself on his favourite instrument, the harpsichord. His musicians, Ceoltóirí Chualann, were highly talented individualists, whom he drilled into a disciplined and harmonious ensemble. The songs, sung by Seán Ó Sé, would often have an introduction by Ó Riada himself, setting them in the historical context of their time. For this alone, 'Reacaireacht an Riadaigh' and 'Fleá Cheoil an Radio' became a one-stop, one-shop master class on the place of Irish music and song in the national story. To hear Seán Ó Sé sing 'Príosún Chluain Meala' or 'Táimse im Chodladh is ná Dúistear Mé' to the accompaniment of Ceoltóirí Chualann following Ó Riada's introduction was far more than an exercise in tuneful accompaniment and singing; it was a richly educational experience, an intravenous injection of the very essence of Irishness, something which, in the most basic sense of the word, re-created the soul.

So when his friend Tom Kinsella, with whom I started this memoir, comments to me that Seán 'has gone all native', I think I know what he means. But, as yet, 'going all native' has not gone as far as it will soon go—when he tells us that night in the Abbey that he is pulling up the roots and going off on another of his safari runs, this time to Clochar, near the village of Ballyferriter in west Kerry. That is early summer 1963; a few months later—I have certainly caught some of the infection from him—I find myself there too, but, unlike Seán, only for a short holiday.

During that time I will sometimes meet him out walking alone or with Ruth, avoiding the company of the 'stróinséaraí', the holiday visitors; even more, the pubs and pub talk with folk who were big on plans but small on actions. He had left all that behind him in Dublin and was not going to fall into the same trap now. What he wanted was what would restore his roots and start up a whole new creative life in him. When I hear him talk like this, I am reminded of Elgar, fled to the northern moors, despairing at the thought of his sublime music being put to jingoistic words:

'Land of hope and glory, Mother of the free'

reminded too—since this is the man who has made music of epic proportions out of 'Róisín Dubh', 'the little black rose of Ireland'—of the Scots poet Hugh Mac Diarmid writing of the imperilled culture of *his* people: 'Not for me the great flowers of all the world; for me the little white rose of Scotland, that smells sweetly and breaks the heart.'

One day he brings the family over to visit ours in our hideout in Emila. There, he points out to me the bars and sturdy wooden shutters on the windows. It had in its time, he tells me, been a bailiff's house, one of the bailiffs of the Earls of Kenmare, the south Kerry planter landlords. Bailiffs did things in those years that were not to people's liking and the bars and shutters were a necessary part of their self-defence. Local lore lives long in such places, and Seán had the story of this particular house from one of the local men—perhaps his friend, the 'sean-nós' singer Seán de hÓra, with whom the Ó Riadas were living at the time. The house had had what he called 'mallacht na baintrí' put on it—the widow's curse. The bailiff, out on one of his rent-collecting forays, had come to this widow's house, where she and her children were assembled about the pot on the earthen floor eating their meagre diet of potatoes and buttermilk. There is no money for the rent, so the bailiff in a rage stamps his muddy boots on the potatoes, squashing them into inedible muck; whereupon the unfortunate widow puts 'mallacht na baintrí' on him, its potent spell ensuring that his seed will die out and his name never again be heard in those parts.

Now, it is indeed a fact that the house had long since fallen into other hands and was no longer owned by anyone of the bailiff's name. But, being the natural-born sceptic I am, I tend not to place much store upon such old wives' tales. Clearly, Seán does. For the first time, I begin to really see what Tom Kinsella had in mind when he told me that Seán had 'gone all native'.

Towards the end of our time in Ballyferriter, Seán came into the village more often, and we would sometimes meet at midday in Dónall Ó Catháin's pub. I can see him now, sitting on a bar stool in the far corner, drinking his single glass of Guinness and reading *The Irish Times*. Compared to their big rambling place in Stillorgan, the space they had in Seán de hÓra's was tight, but the company was good, de hÓra himself being a daily creative source with his knowledge of the rich local lore and his passionate singing of the great songs—'Bean Dubh a Ghleanna', 'Beinnsín Luachra' and 'An Brianach Óg'. Living in the same house together for much of that year, Ó Riada, through him, came in touch with a deep seam of native cultural riches, ice packed for centuries but still alive in the voices of Corca Dhuibhne now daily in his ears. This would be the abiding influence in his life from then on, the lodestar he would follow for the rest of his days.

How Ruth managed to run the household in such cramped conditions is indeed a mystery; but run it she did and with style and energy too. Always with the Ó Riadas there were the signs and symbols of high culture about: the bookracks, the records, the cassettes and sound equipment— odd bedfellows in a cottier's house in a backward place.

But, God, what a scene confronted you when you came out the door—the thunderous Atlantic pounding the beach below; that 'roaring wave tormenting me as I woke' of the eighteenth-century poet Aogán Ó Rathaille; one of the Blaskets, a giant reclining out on the horizon; Ceann Sibéal and the Three Sisters away to the north; Márthain and Ceann Sratha to the south; and majestic Brandon, named from Kerry's saint, Brendan the Navigator, towering above the flat lands in towards Dingle—a tumultuous, awe-inspiring sight, flung down by the hand of God the day creation began! It is, without doubt, one of the great epic landscapes of the world.

The scenery is one thing; only a clod or a sod could not but be touched by it. But it is the people there that Seán came to love. There he is, with his wife and young family, come among them as a stranger; yet after no more than a few months he is completely at home—a modern Rip Van Winkle reabsorbed into a life and culture that were quintessentially his own, but of which his people had been dispossessed long centuries before.

On the very last day of my time there, I go into Ó Catháin's as usual and there he is, sitting on his bar stool, his single glass of Guinness before him. When I tell him I am leaving, he looks at me out of his cavalier eyes—at the time he is 'high' on the poetry of Piaras Feiritéar, the bandit-prince hanged in Killarney in 1653, when one of the great plantations that drove out the native nobility was at its height. I rather think Seán may have seen in himself an inheritor and a defender of that princely past, restored now to honour and respect among his own; and I like to flatter myself into thinking he saw in me—that Bill Murphy he had known in Cork long before, and in the young Irish-speaking family I now had about me—someone in the same mould, someone who in adult years had discovered what a pearl of great price we had in our native language, which had by now become central to both our lives.

'Níl tú ag dul aon áit,' he tells me with a toss of his handsome head. 'Tá tú ag fanúint anseo.'

I protest that I cannot stay, that our rented house in Emila has been let to someone else; whereupon he tells me, even more defiantly, that that doesn't matter; he will find us another place.

What follows, as we stop at every third or fourth house between there and Dún Chaoin, is a riot of songs, music and poetry, of old stories with new friends, a voyage of discovery into what is for me a rich and exciting new world, a world that will nurture and replenish me for the rest of my days. At last he finds us the accommodation we need and it is a fortnight later before we finally part. This time, it is after dinner with the Ó Riadas, alchemised with culinary skill by Ruth from things all locally produced, with me promising faithfully to read the poems of Piaras Feiritéar, and Seán the major new history of the Famine, *The Great Hunger* by Cecil Woodham-Smith, then just out. We arrange to meet in Dublin in a month when he will be up for the next recording of 'Fleá Cheoil an Radio'. Other promises are made, other undertakings given, all lavish and all heartfelt;

there had been some drink taken! Our devoted wives look at each other in mutual dismay; it is as well perhaps that from now on we will be hundreds of miles apart!

On that final day of our time in Ballyferriter, Seán does what professionals rarely do—he plays some music. This is in Kruger Kavanagh's pub in Dún Chaoin. There are several people about who know, and whose people before them knew, the great songs in Irish, some of them centuries old; here now is this 'blow-in' among them who began to learn those songs the day before yesterday! The air he plays is 'Mo Mhúirnín Bán', an air he had used as the theme music for the Four Provinces film of Synge's *The Playboy of the Western World*.

We have all heard great whistle players in our time: Paddy Maloney of the Chieftains and Seán Potts are among them; as are Cathal McConnell of the Boys of the Lough and Mary Bergin of Dordán in Galway. But no whistle player I have ever heard will equal the rapture of Ó Riada's playing on that day. The words tell in music a simple story, the story of young love, desperate love, love lost and love regained, the whole demented cycle of that most elemental of human emotions:

> *Do bhí mé oíche na Féile Bríde*
> *Ag an aonach thíos ar an Mullach Mór;*
> *Nuair a dhearc mé an fhaoileann dar thug mé gnaoi di,*
> *Ó, is í do bhí aoibhinn, geal, áluinn, óg.*

It is an air that will be locked for ever in my memory with the memory of Seán that day in what must surely have been the happiest period of his short life. Not long after that, Dún Chaoin, 'Mo Mhúirnín Bán' and the thrilling discovery of a new flowering in his own and his family's life would be in the past, a past over which, as yet, no clouds had gathered but the clouds at sunset spreading above Brandon and Ceann Sibéil.

By the time the next year comes around, 1964, I have left the civil service and gone to work in RTÉ; Seán has left the safe haven of Clochar and has gone to live near the village of Cúil Aodha in west Cork. From there he commutes the forty-odd miles daily to a lectureship in Professor Aloys Fleischmann's Music Department of UCC. For yet one more time he has a steady job; along with it, he has the weekly 'Fleá Cheoil an Radio'; there are other assignments as well, some quite lucrative. For perhaps the first time in his life he is making some real money. When he comes to Dublin he stays in the opulent Shelbourne or with his friend, scion of the Guinness house, Garech de Brún.

On one such foray to Dublin, he does this Christmas television programme with Ceoltóirí Chualann for RTÉ. The producer of the programme is a talented man with some good credits to his name, but patience and forbearance with the ways and foibles of other creative souls are not among them. Whatever difference comes between them, fireworks break out and Seán, not the most forbearing of people himself, stalks out of the studio, stubbornly refusing to come back until an apology is made. There is no apology. So he goes one better and vows never to perform on RTÉ television again unless and until that apology is forthcoming.

This is the situation when I go to see him in the Shelbourne one day in 1965 to ask him to participate in a new series of traditional music programmes which I am planning. The series is aimed at the average English-speaking viewer, introducing him/her to the substance and beauty of Irish music and song—exactly the kind of thing Seán himself has been doing for years with 'Reacaireacht an Riadaigh' and

'Fleá Cheoil an Radio'. He listens carefully to what I am saying; I add the usual bit about fees, rehearsal arrangements, production and transmission times. When I finish, quietly, courteously, he tells me I am wasting my time.

'Ní dhéanfaidh mé é. Mhasluigh RTÉ mé uair amháin cheana, ní bhfaghaidh siad deis é dhéanamh arís.' (I won't do it. RTÉ insulted me once before. They won't get a chance to do it again.)

The series is one for which I have big hopes. I am very disappointed. What is more, for once I have total support for it in RTÉ—from Gunnar Rugheimer in particular, our Swedish Controller and a great fan of Seán's, who would do anything to get him on. So I wait for a week or so to let my attractive programme idea sink in, as I am sure it will. Then I take myself off down to Cúil Aodha to plead with him again, hoping that my persistence and the trouble I am taking will do the trick.

It is an early summer evening when I arrive. As we drive up to the hilltop pub of Barr a' Choma on the road to Kilgarvan—latterly in the news since the emergence of one Jacky Healy Rae!—we talk about anything and everything but the subject for which I have come. The talk, incidentally, I recall includes another 'first' from Seán: all the way up the mountain road, he sings several verses of 'Scoil Bhard Inse', the local odyssey celebrating the name and fame of everyone who ever did anything in the uncharted world between Kilgarvan and Baile Bhúirne! All through the very pleasant few hours that follow, the television programme is never mentioned. When we come back down, he brings me into his music room to hear the recording he has just made of his latest work-in-progress. It is with a group of local men singing what appears to be religious music, including the eighteenth-century Tadhg Gaelach Ó Súilleabháin's 'Gile mo Chroí do Chroí-se, a Shláinaitheoir'. I do not realise it then, but I believe that was the first time an outsider had heard the now famous 'Aifreann Uí Riada' sung by Cór Chúil Aodha.

Then, at last it is time for me to leave; so I bring up the subject which had brought me. For one thing, I foolishly think that he has surely appreciated that, out of respect for him, I have left it until now; for another, that I have given myself a four hundred mile journey to plead with him! Who does appreciate it is Ruth, who is standing in the hallway with us as I am about to go. But scarcely have I the first word out than he cuts me off.

'Tá mo chuid ráite agam faoin scéal sin', he tells me. 'Níl mé chun aon obair a dhéanamh do RTÉ TV.'

Ruth interjects that it is not RTÉ who is asking him, it is me. Wrongly, as it happens, she goes on to say that in all probability RTÉ doesn't give a damn one way or the other if the programme is never made. But, clearly, I do.

'Tá Liam ag iarraidh rud fónta a dhéanamh don teanga san áit sin,' she says. 'Ar son Dé, ná cabhrófá leis?'

It is no good. So I leave, disappointed. But, before I do, Ruth manages to get to me with a whisper in my ear: 'Imigh leat. Fág é seo fúmsa.'

The following week, Éamon de Buitléar, who acted as secretary to Ceoltóirí Chualann, comes to me with something Seán Ó Riada has given him when he was in Dublin for one of his 'Fleá Cheoil an Radio' recordings. It is a 'Sweet Afton' cigarette packet, slit open and with a list of titles on the white inside. There on top is the title, 'Freedom and the Rights of Man' and, below, eight others—songs, slow airs and dance music. It is the running order for the first programme in the series. Among them are the seventeenth-century Jacobite song, 'Seán Ó Duibhir a' Ghleanna';

'Maidin Luain Cincíse' and 'Sliabh na mBan' from the 1798 Rising; some harp pieces from the blind O'Carolan and Ruairí Dall Ó Catháin; and a jig, 'Freedom and the Rights of Man', dating from the period of Tom Paine's pamphlet of that title, which had been a kind of manifesto for the French Revolution. With the splendid visual material we dig out for the programme—press cuttings, stills, archive clips—it turns out to be a superb production, a mini *Mise Éire* in its own right! And 'Aililiú', as the series is called, is off to a mighty start.

The following day, I get a phone call from Geneva, where they had just arrived at a European Broadcasting Union meeting, from RTÉ Director General Kevin McCourt and Programme Controller Gunnar Rugheimer to say that they had seen the programme the night before and greatly admired it; and to enquire what charm or witchcraft I had used to get Ó Riada on.

'It wasn't me,' I said, 'it was a woman.'

'Oh? Is Seán that way inclined?'

'Indeed, he is,' I tell them. 'She is a woman he usually finds it hard to resist!'

So now we have the beginnings of a reconciliation between Seán and RTÉ but, more menacingly, we have the beginnings of other things as well. For, from then on, he becomes something of a popular celebrity, not just the Seán Ó Riada of musical fame, but a television personality in the wider field.

Producer Jack Dowling, a man of considerable, if unorthodox, talent in his own right, has him as presenter and interviewer on an arts programme, 'Insight'; there he surprises us all by the range of his knowledge and, even more, by his elegant dress and linguistic skills. On one programme, during the Dublin Theatre Festival, he conducts the interviews with perfect fluency in four languages—Irish, English, French and German, the latter with some delightful young people from the cast of the Black Theatre of Prague—all with quickfire translations for the benefit of English-speaking folk. He turns out to be wholly at ease in a television studio, his elegant tweeds and long cheroots bearing the stamp and mark of some well-endowed savant from the Left Bank of the Seine, temporarily gone astray on the highways and byways of west Cork! Later again, one of the producers, Seán Ó Mórdha, does a splendid traditional music series with him which should surely have been the first of many but for the way his life then began to go. Shortly after the transmission of that series, RTÉ, in its haste to clear the videotape library, had it summarily wiped—a lesson, some unloving critic said, in the grim truth that one should not cast pearls before swine!

What we have then is yet another Seán Ó Riada, an instant success in front of camera, largely because he scarcely noticed that cameras were there. Aloof and haughty he can be when he choses; but then again, he can turn on the charm to become close and intimate and bring out the very best in his interviewee. Occasionally also, there will be touches of a kind of studied folksiness—as when, coming to studio at festive times, he will have a bottle of well-matured Cúil Aodha poitín wrapped in a newspaper under his arm. 'Pour les amitiés', he will say, or 'Mar chomhartha measa ort.' This can have an ironic, but quite delightful side to it: once, for a Christmas chat-show, he arrives in a taxi with the peace offering from Cúil Aodha as usual under his arm. Hospitality has been laid on for the post-programme session, but he insists on us having a drink from his bottle first before the 'purchased' drink is touched. Among our guests on the show is George Colley, then Minister for Finance—the minister responsible for customs and excise, including the excise on drink. But the illegal poitín stands above the man-made law of the land: it is bound by the more imperative Irish law, that of hospitality among neighbours. It would be churlish, uncivilised—above all it would be 'frith-Ghaelach' (un-Irish)—to refuse such a 'comhartha measa' from a man from Cúil Aodha.

The poitín, alas, may have given an early hint of another story. Now, after all the years, I don't suppose I am betraying any secrets by saying that drink would be the ruin of that most talented man. With time, it became worse. Some few years before he died, he was warned off it totally because of a liver ailment—a stricture he did not heed. Some loyal friends tried to help, but either he could not see that he needed help, or he was too headstrong to accept it; in either case, it would become a rapid descent from then on.

Once in an effort to get him back into his classical composition mode, I arrange that he get a contract for a full-scale work which he had been talking about for some time. This was an oratorio to be perfomed on the occasion of the death—whenever that might be—of President de Valera, like himself, a Limerick man whom he greatly admired and who, in turn, greatly admired him. The details were worked out with his former colleague, RTÉ's Director of Music, Gerard Victory: 'Requiem for a Dead Leader' would be its title; it would be in three parts; the RTÉ Symphony Orchestra and Our Lady's Choral Society would perform it. Part 1 was indeed started and seemed to give some semblance of promise; but it never got further than that. Parts 2 and 3 never even got that far.

During all this time, he continues to commute the forty-odd miles from Cúil Aodha to UCC, with drink an increasing daily menace. One day, on his way there, he stops at the Millíní pub in Baile Bhúirne where, a while later, a good friend finds him leaning against the wall much the worse for wear. The friend remonstrates with him for what he is doing to himself, wasting in pubs and on drink the most gifted talent the country has. Far gone as he is, Seán's response is as savagely direct as it is tragic: 'Any talent I had is dried up. Any good work I had to do was done a long time ago.' It is the testament of a realist who has lost the hope that drink might help him reach the sublime heights he had reached long ago.

Clearly, by then he was in need of medical care, probably institutional; even more so, some panacea was necessary to lift from his darkening soul the conviction that his life was going nowhere, and in the process that he was dragging down, not just himself, but his beloved wife and family. The aloof, distant, aristocratic Seán was now gone, and what remained was but a shadow, barely recognisable, a man who was weeping inside; a weeping, his friend Len Clifford would say, that made others cry; a weeping that was too grievous to last, too wounding not to touch the stoutest heart.

And so he dies and we bury him at last in Reilig Ghobnatan in Baile Bhúirne—anonymous thousands of us who were touched to the depths of our souls by the music of this gifted man. Ruth will soon join him—the life they had known together was surely over once Seán was gone. Some time after his death, I get RTÉ to commission a head of him, done by his good friend, the sculptor, Séamus Murphy. It is set on a plinth in one of the patio gardens of RTÉ's Radio Centre, a strong, bold head, the head of a countryman—not the elegant, cavalier head of Seán Ó Riada of earlier times living it up on the Left Bank in Paris, more the self-reliant pilgrim father forging a new life, a new consciousness for himself in Clochar, Ballyferriter and the fastnesses of west Cork.

Was it a mistake for him ever to have come back? Would he, like those other Irish wayfarers—Joyce, O'Casey, Beckett—have done better to have stayed away, to live out his life 'in silence, exile, cunning'? Who knows? Is there any other life for any of us but the one we live; any other choice but the one we make; that pre-ordination of our unique destiny, the one and only destiny we can ever call our own? For Seán, whatever its shortcomings, whatever its later faults and failings, it had to have been a good life. For him, however long or short its years, it was surely true that 'those whom the gods love die young'.

To us, to the Ireland he left behind, he bequeathed a distinction and an excellence which drew us nearer to the kind of people we can be; to an elegance, style and quality of mind and soul which are quintessentially Irish, Irish to the core. His Cúil Aodha friend, Peaití Thaidhg Pheig, had said to him as he lay dying: 'Fad atáimid beo, a Sheáin, caithfimid a bheith Gaelach.' (While we're alive, we must be Irish.) Seán would tell me that story again and again in his last years. It is the brand-mark with which we face our judgment and our eternity.

In Czarist Russia a hundred years before his time, that tormented man, Nikolai Gogol, would write a story, 'The Overcoat', which would become the forerunner for all the great Russian literature that followed. Some time later, his fellow countryman, Anton Chekhov—master of the short story—would say: 'We all came out from under Gogol's "Overcoat".' Of the traditional music of Ireland, right down to the world-wide success of the Chieftains, 'Riverdance',

'Lord of the Dance' and all the rest, the same may truly be said: they all came out from under the overcoat of Seán Ó Riada. Solas na bhflaitheas dá anam uasal; agus do anam a bheanchéile dílis. Tá sean-chultúr na hÉireann buíoch daoibh.

Rider from the Sea

SIOBHÁN McKENNA

When I came back to RTÉ from my producer-training course at the BBC in 1964, one of the first tasks that faced me was to devise a set of Irish language-teaching programmes. These would be aimed, not so much at people without any Irish, as at the majority of the population who had some residual Irish from their schooldays and, for one reason or another, wanted to brush up on it, usually so as to be able to help their children. Being neither a teacher nor, less still, a linguistic expert, language-teaching programmes were about the very last thing I wanted to do; my aim at the time would have been to create programmes, both in Irish and bilingual, which people would want to watch for their entertainment or enlightenment value, rather than for some dull pedagogic reason, of which they had had far too much at school. But the RTÉ Authority, in particular that dour but committed language enthusiast Ernest Blythe, wanted the lessons, and I was the man in the gap to provide them. Such lessons had been successfully done on radio in the past but never on television; some preliminary work had been undertaken which seemed to suggest that there weren't the acting or production people, or the writing skills, to make them. The man I chose to advise me on the linguistics side was a brilliant and mercurial Franciscan, pathfinder to much subsequent linguistic development in Ireland, Father Colmán Ó Huallacháin. He had been a professor of philosophy in the national seminary in Maynooth, but following a palace upheaval he had been chucked out and ended up on a linguistics fellowship in Canada and the US, where he came under the influence of some renowned scholars—Joshua Fishman, Walter Lambert and Noam Chomsky.

His first advice to me was that, whatever television method we used, we would have to have as a front person to present the programme someone with clear, standardised Irish—the equivalent of what used to be known as 'BBC English'. When I asked who that might be, without a second's hesitation he said, 'Siobhán McKenna.'

As things turned out, the teaching programme we did devise, 'Labhair Gaeilge Linn', did not have Siobhán; in the then poorly endowed Irish language department of RTÉ, we would probably never have been able to rise to her performance fees; besides, having become the international name she then was—she had just recently played the lead role in *The Playboy of the Western World* and a secondary role in David Lean's *Dr Zhivago*—she would simply not have been available to do a weekly television show. So in her place the name we came up with was a rumbustious but lovable Oliver Reed of a man who was with the Abbey Theatre at the time, Eoin Ó Súilleabháin.

Eoin's Irish was a rich blend of Kerry and Connemara— his father, Muiris Ó Súilleabháin, author of *Fiche Bliain Ag Fás*, had a foot in both camps. Siobhán would later congratulate me on making such a splendid choice. 'Ní chuirfinn leath an oiread croí ann is a chuireann Eoinín', she generously conceded. (I wouldn't put half the heart into it which Eoin does.) Anyone who saw his trajectory and panache in front of camera would be bound to agree.

I was to know her husband, Denis O'Dea, long before I got to know Siobhán. He was one of a strange if erudite coterie around a sage-figure in Dalkey, Paddy Darcy. As a boy of 16, Darcy, son of an RIC man, had taken his father's gun and his bicycle and cycled into Dublin to be with the insurgents in 1916. Denis O'Dea had in his time had a rub of the militant relic and, true to form, would continue throughout his life to be a strongly republican-minded man. But that part of his life was over now; the shooting he now favoured was with film and, as with another pair of Dalkey luminaries, Dan and Michael O'Herlihy (*Hawaii Five-O*) it looked for a time as if he might make it big in Hollywood. But once Siobhán entered his life, his focus changed and he became an extraordinarily staid and settled husband— although Paddy Darcy would always say he was not the man to cross when his dander was up!

It was by chance that I was to hear that he and Siobhán were husband and wife. This was when I learned that they were among 'the first of the few' parents to send their only child, Donncha, to the newly founded all-Irish school in Monkstown, Scoil Lorcáin. There were twenty-two children in that first ever Scoil Lorcáin, located in a single room above the public library in Blackrock Town Hall—among them also the daughters of Maureen and Cyril Cusack, Sinéad and Sorcha.

'Gaelscoileanna' have sprung up everywhere since. Sending a child from an English-speaking home to an all-Irish school has now become quite the thing; but at that time, forty-five years ago, it was taking a big chance with the child's formation. Only a deep commitment to the language and the culture it contained could lead parents to do it. I cannot say for certain where the major influence came from in the case of the Cusack girls and Donncha O'Dea, but I rather suspect that in both cases it was from the fathers, both of them, Cyril and Denis, strongly nationalist, and with a profound feeling for the language, even though they themselves did not speak it well. In this they were exemplars of what Cyril would later refer to as 'the doubting Thomas syndrome': 'Blessed are they, Thomas, who have not seen and have believed.' In any case, off the kids go to that single classroom above Blackrock Town Hall—a tiny seed from which the giant tree of the 'Gaelscoileanna' movement has now grown. Rarely can an 'upper room' have had such long-term effects!

So Franciscan Father Colmán's dream of having Siobhán present 'Labhair Gaeilge Linn' does not come to pass; but that is not the end of the story so far as I am concerned. For, every year from then on, I put together a set of Christmas pieces—stories, poems, snatches of autobiography—and in a small set in the tiny Studio 3 Siobhán comes in to present them. Mícheál Mac Liammóir, Cyril Cusack and she are the three best-known names in Irish theatre at that time; the idea of one of them coming in to do a show in Irish in the smallest, least-equipped studio in RTÉ would be unthinkable—a big rig with a full crew in the copious Studio 1 would be nearer the mark. But those Christmas shows with Siobhán, with just an armchair and a table-lamp, become gems of intimate, highly personalised television. In one of them, she reads a piece from Peig, the autobiography of Blasket Islander Peig Sayers. It is the Christmas scene where the little 12-year-old girl is in service with a well-off family in Dingle. As they light the Christmas candle and the children run about the floor screaming with delight, hugging and kissing their mother, she cannot help thinking of her own mother, alone in the little thatched cottage on their windswept island. It is surely one of the most poignant pieces of reminiscence ever written, close in its way to Maxim Gorki's memories of his grandmother in Czarist Russia, or those of the orphaned New Englander, Mary McCarthy, in *Memories of a Catholic Childhood*. Disciplined and professional performer as she was, Siobhán would find it difficult to keep her voice from breaking as she read it.

Ansin, d'éirigh Neil agus thug sí léi trí shórt aráin agus ghearr amach é ar mhéis. Bhí subh agus im go flúirseach ar an mbord. Nuair a bhí na soilse go léir lasta agus an chistin déanta suas, tuigeadh domsa go rabhas ar neamh, mar a leithéid sin de radharc ní fhaca roimhe sin riamh. Scaoil Neil amach an tae is shuigh gach duine chun boird. Bhíodar go léir go pléisiúrtha agus go gealgháireach, go mórmhór Neil. Níl aon chor a chuireadh an chlann díobh ná go gcuireadh sé lúcháir uirthi. Bhíos féin ag féachaint orthu agus á dtabhairt fé ndeara is mé ag ól mo chuid tae. Rith smaointe isteach i m'aigne; ar mo mháthair bhocht a smaoiníos san am sin. Bhí fhios agam conas mar a bhí an oíche aici ina hainniseoir dorcha uaigneach gan sólás gan suáilceas, mar is mise an t-aon sólás amháin a bhí aici. Bhíos i bhfad uaithi anois, agus níorbh fhéidir liom aon tógaint chroí ná meidhir a chur uirthi.

'Is ait é toisc an tsaoil,' arsa mise liom féin. 'Féach Neil agus an compord atá aici á bhaint as a clainn, agus máithreacha bochta eile gan aon phioc de shólás an tsaoil acu.' Tháinig na deora le mo shúile dá mhéad compord a bhí timpeall orm.

(Then Nell got up and brought three kinds of bread to the table and cut them up on the plate. There was plenty of butter and jam and, when the lights were lit and the kitchen done up, I thought I was in heaven, because a sight like it I had never seen before. Nell poured out the tea and everyone sat down. They were all so happy and pleased with each other, especially Nell. Every move one of the family made delighted her. I was looking at them and taking it all in as I drank the tea. And I began to think; of my own poor mother I was thinking then. I knew how this night would be with her, a poor creature all alone in a dark place, without solace or happiness because I was the one solace in the world she had. And I was far away from her and could do nothing now to brighten her life.

'Isn't it a sad world,' I said to myself. 'Look at Nell there and all the happiness she has from her family around her. And other poor mothers with no happiness in the world at all.' And the tears came, in spite of all the comforts I had around me.)

Donncha O'Dea, son of Siobhán and Denis, would later make a name for himself as an international swimmer; the swimming columns in the sports pages were constantly featuring him. So I think to myself that it will make a good story if I can get some of the family together on an after-dinner TV chat-show running at the time, 'Iarphroinn'.

Siobhán agrees, as does her sister Nancy. Donncha's prowess is enough to have him there in his own right; but since you cannot swim and talk at the same time, certainly not at international level, not much talk is expected from him! Which is just as well; when the girls get going, he is not going to get a word in anyway. But what talk it is—the ease, the clarity, the sheer perfection of their scholarly, educated

Irish.

Colmán Ó Huallacháin had indeed been right: if we were ever going to have a standardised form of spoken Irish, something that would be instantly understood in every Gaeltacht, from Donegal to Connemara to Kerry, Cork and Ring, this surely was it. It so impresses me that I ask them about it in the hospitality suite afterwards. Their response, as I remember it, is interesting, if for no other reason than to show how the atmosphere in which a language is learned in a child's growing years can affect the whole learning process afterwards.

Their father, a Corkman, had taught maths/physics for a time in Queen's in Belfast, where Siobhán was born; he later moved to a similar job in University College Galway. Their mother, as I remember, did not speak Irish all that well, but she had the essential thing—she was a willing learner. How come then that the girls spoke it perfectly? It was, they said, because of the way things happened at home: whenever the atmosphere was good and they were all happy together, the language was Irish; when things went wrong and the atmosphere was bad, it turned over to English, an unconscious, light-and-shade oscillation which, half a lifetime later, could still produce models of linguistic perfection. What a pity that that simple lesson in language engineering has never been learnt by the educational savants!

About Siobhán McKenna's acting life, apart from what is generally known, I have very little to say. Though there are perhaps one or two things. One of them is about Foley's of Inch, a fine pub. It is within walking distance of Inch Strand, surely one of the great stretches of golden sand in the world.

It spans the top of the inlet between the two great peninsulas of Kerry, Corcha Dhuibhne to the north and Uíbh Rathach to the south, with the magnificent peaks vying with each other for the honours of the 'Kingdom': Carrantouhill and the McGillacuddy Reeks above Killarney, and Brandon shouldering its way into the Atlantic above Cuas Bhréanainn.

It was there, in a little hovel near Inch, that the seventeenth-century poet Aogán Ó Rathaille wrote some of the most elemental verses ever written against the destruction of the ancient Irish civilisation by new conquerors:

Do leathnaigh an ciach diachrach fám sheana-chroí dúr
ar thaisteal na ndiabhal n-iasachta I bhfearann Choinn chughainn;
scamall ar ghriain iarthair dár cheartas ríocht Mumhan
fá deara dhom triall riamh ort, a Vailintín Brún.

That my old bitter heart was pierced in this black doom,
That foreign devils have made our land a tomb,
That the sun that was Munster's glory has gone down
Has made me a beggar before you, Valentine Brown.

Caiseal gan cliar, fiailteach ná macraí ar dtúis
is beanna-bhruig Bhriain ciarthuilte, 'mhadraíbh úisc,
Ealla gan triar triaithe de mhacaibh rí Mumhan
fá deara dhom triall riamh ort, a Vailintín Brún.

That royal Cashel is bare of house and guest,
That Brian's turreted home is the otter's nest,
That the kings of the land have neither land nor crown
Has made me a beggar before you, Valentine Brown.

Translation: Frank O'Connor

This was the location chosen for the outdoor sequences in the Four Provinces film production of Synge's *The Playboy of the Western World*, in which Siobhán played the role of Pegeen Mike. The music score was done by Seán Ó Riada with his traditional ensemble, Ceoltóirí Chualann (later to become the backbone of the Chieftains). At the end of each day's shoot, cast and crew would repair to Foley's of Inch for a great night's 'ceol, craic agus comhrá'.

To this day—it is all of forty years ago—the people around those parts, those still alive, remember those days and nights, in particular, the coming together of two of the most seminal names in the Irish language and cultural scene of that time— Seán Ó Riada and Siobhán McKenna. Siobhán had made her debut in the Irish language theatre, Taibhdhearc na Gaillimhe where, as a student in UCG, she had come under the influence of Mícheál Mac Liammóir and Hilton Edwards during their time there. Author and actor Walter Macken was also a member of that company, as was a remarkable and scholarly Dubliner, back in time from a German university to be in the Royal College of Surgeons under Countess Markievicz in 1916, Professor Liam Ó Briain. All that, together with her happy experience with the language in her own home, made her a very receptive companion for Seán Ó Riada, whose growing love affair with the language was coming into focus then.

Seán's reputation as a composer of film music was well established with the *Mise Éire* and *Saoirse* scores of the early 1960s; but he was deep into the native tradition when the Four Provinces film people commissioned him for the *Playboy* score. So it was no surprise to anyone that he should choose the traditional mode. Great nights of music and set-dancing took place in Foley's then, interspersed with those periods of rapt attention while one of the slow airs was being sung or played: someone like Seán Potts on the whistle with 'Sé Fáth Mo Bhuartha' or Seán de hÓra in from Clochar singing 'An Brianach Og'. This in turn would give way to great rounds of Kerry slides and set-dances. 'Oh, the days of the Kerry dancing' it was then all right, freshly minted in the coin of the romantic, Christy Mahon honey-mouthing his irascible Pegeen Mike, fiercely jealous of the other girls' attempts to catch the Playboy's eye.

Pegeen: Yourself and me would shelter easy in a narrow bush. But we're only talking, maybe, for this would be a poor thatched place to hold a fine lad is the like of you.

Christy: If I wasn't a good Christian, it's on my naked knees I'd be, saying me prayers and paters to every jackstraw you have roofing your head, and every stony pebble is paving the laneway to your door.

Pegeen: If that's the truth, I'll be burning candles from this day out to the miracles of God that have brought you from the south today, and I with my gowns bought ready, the way I can wed you, and not wait at all.

Christy: It's miracles, and that's the truth. Me there toiling a long while, and walking a long while, not knowing at all I was drawing at all times nearer to this holy day.

Pegeen: And myself, a girl, was tempted often to go sailing the seas till I'd marry a Jew-man, with ten kegs of gold, and I not knowing at all there was the like of you drawing nearer, like the stars of God.

The sleeve on the old wax disc with Ó Riada's music, which I have before me as I write, shows Siobhán on tiptoe on the strand, all kitted out in red petticoat and shawl, with a mane of auburn hair above a face wistful and dreaming. It is stylised all right, more sophisticated than the original Pegeen

Mike could ever have been. But Siobhán herself would have been well familiar with such a kit from her Galway years, as she would surely have been with the scene in that haunting air with which Ó Riada introduced the film, 'Mo Mhúirnín Bán':

> Do bhí mé oíche na Féile Bríde
> Ag an aonach thíos ar an Mullach Mór,
> Nuair a dhearc mé an fhaoileann dar thug mé gnaoi di,
> Ó, sí do bhí aoibhinn, geal, áluinn, óg.

The Playboy did not make a big box-office success; it would take a David Lean and a budget a hundred times the *Playboy*'s to make a success of a much lesser story, *Ryan's Daughter*, shot on the same magnificent peninsula years later. But its failure had nothing to do with Siobhán, for she was surely the perfect prototype for whom the part of Pegeen Mike might well have been written in the first place.

What was more surprising was the less than usual success of Brian Friel's play, *The Loves of Cass Maguire*, in which she also played the lead role. Cass, an ageing spinster, is back from years in the States, with just about enough to settle down and live out the last of her days back home in Ireland. But she is a garrulous old windbag, constantly caught between extremes of booze and sentimentality; there is no way she will be happy in the closed society of the Ireland to which she returns.

In the midst of the gin-swilling and boisterous garrulity, she is given to wild extremes of grief and rage, a manic concoction that will surely land her up in some coronary care unit or neurosurgical ward.

It was a powerful and heartfelt performance by Siobhán—

were there some real Cass Maguires in her own life whose crises she was re-enacting? One could see those crises coming several times in the course of the play, when she would blow the gasket-head off and fall down dead there in our very presence.

I go to see her in her dressing-room afterwards and tell her what a stupendous performance it has been, leaving us all stunned, pole-axed, with pity and terror. And there she is, easy as you like, knocking back gin and tonics, looking as if she has never been out there at all! How does she take the strain, I ask. Is she not coming to a time in life when such a tumultuous performance will be beyond her? No, she says with a toss of her head, she is not; it is the one thing in the world she wants to do; she loves it and will continue to do it until she drops. I think of Gerard Manley Hopkins's phrase 'A man's inscape is his sanity' ('inscape', the opposite of 'escape'). In this respect Siobhán McKenna *is* Pegeen Mike, *is* Cass Maguire, as years before in Taibhdhearc na Gaillimhe she *was* Shaw's St Joan, and, down through the years, all the great women characters great dramatists ever created, so that she might take their part.

The last programme we do together is a 'Trom agus Éadrom' celebrating the 25th anniversary of Scoil Lorcáin where her son Donncha had started school. This happens to coincide with the establishment of 'Fondúireacht an Phiarsaigh' (the Pearse Foundation), an annual award for outstanding service to the Irish language and culture. The programme itself is the usual mix of entertainment, audience participation and talk. But what I remember best about it were two wholly spontaneous renderings of poems by Pearse. The first, done by Siobhán herself, 'The Fool', was, she said, a blueprint for

Irish independence and what would follow it down through the generations:

The lawyers have sat in council, the men with the keen long faces,
And said, 'This man is a fool', and others have said, 'He
   blasphemeth';
And the wise have pitied the fool that hath striven to give a life
In the world of time and space among the bulks of actual things,
To a dream that was dreamed in the heart, and that only the heart
   could hold.
O wise men, riddle me this: what if the dream come true?
What if the dream come true? And if millions unborn shall dwell
In the house that I shaped in my heart, the noble house of my
   thought?

The second poem, 'The Rebel', wholly unexpected, wholly unrehearsed, was recited by Éamonn de Barra, a friend of the Pearse family and himself a veteran of 1916. He was an old man then and just happened to be sitting in the audience when Siobhán said her piece. 'The Fool', he said, should never be read without reading 'The Rebel' at the same time, their basic message being the same:

And I say to my people's masters: Beware,
Beware of the thing that is coming, beware of the risen people,
Who shall take what ye would not give. Did ye think to conquer
   the people
Or that Law is stronger than life and than men's desire to be free?

To finish where Siobhán would almost certainly want me to finish—with another of Synge's Aran plays. I never did see her playing Maurya in *Riders to the Sea*; but with that full-throated Galway voice coming in gigantic waves from the wild Atlantic, she was surely the matrix from which all succeeding versions of Synge's Aran women were struck. As they bring the last of her sons up from the Claddagh, wrapped in a torn sail, that aboriginal Irish voice comes riding in from the sea along with it:

'They're all gone now, and there isn't anything more the sea can do to me. I'll have no call now to be up crying and praying when the wind breaks from the south, and you can hear the surf is in the east and the surf is in the west, making a great stir with the two noises and they hitting one on the other. I'll have no call now to be going down and getting Holy Water in the dark nights after Samhain, and I won't care what way the sea is when the other women will be keening.'

The keening for Siobhán is over; the curtain has come down. With her great-hearted spirit will go the blessing that went with Sarsfield's 'Wild Geese' long centuries before her time: Go dté tú, a mhúirnín, slán.

Enfant (not so!) Terrible

SEÁN MACENTEE

Growing up in Cork during the war years, the only time one might see Seán MacEntee was on an election platform. Whenever that happened, there were bound to be ructions. Something about his name seemed to bring out the worst in people, admittedly anti-Fianna Fáil people who, from the Civil War years and the bitterness that followed, were not exactly de Valera fans!

An anecdote from that time has the mother of her illegitimate son being asked by the priest what name she wants to christen him; and being understandably shocked when she says, 'Seán MacEntee', she adds: 'If you can think of a better name for a bastard than that, you're smarter than I am!'

Nor was that only in Cork, stronghold of Fine Gael's W. T. (Willie) Cosgrave. Food rationing had been introduced early on in the war, a skilfully organised scheme in difficult circumstances which would see the country through hard times. The chief architect for this was the specially appointed Minister for Supplies, Seán Lemass; yet, in a popular adaptation of a music hall number of the time, it is Seán MacEntee who incurs the odium:

> *Bless 'em all, bless 'em all,*
> *The long and the short and the tall,*
> *Bless de Valera and Seán MacEntee,*
> *Who gave us brown bread and the half ounce of tea;*

Sure, they rationed the cocoa and all,
But they aren't rationed at all,
They're bringing starvation to our little nation,
So turn to St Vincent de Paul.

In the Fianna Fáil final rally in Cork before the 1945 general election, MacEntee was billed as their lead-speaker and some pretty hefty action was expected. This was a time when elections were fought out in the public arena, not on radio and television as they are now. Election rallies, with the annual church missions, were the big crowd-pullers of those years. On this night, Patrick Street is packed, mostly with party aficionados, but with a sizeable admixture of antagonists too who would guarantee a fine fracas later on.

Bear in mind that this is but a short few years since the guns were out in Marsh's mart-yard during a Blueshirt/IRA row about the ban on the sale of cattle to Britain, a ban predictably devised by the cloven-hoofed de Valera and grandiosely known as the 'Economic War'. During that time, Seán MacEntee had been Minister for Finance, and many a farmer in Cork and further afield would gladly have had his guts for garters for his part in the economic plight they were in. So with the more pugilistic of the Blueshirt faction in the wings that night, a lively session was predicted.

When eventually the fighting breaks out, it spreads like wildfire until, at one point, it looks as if the whole crowd will be involved. The vortex seems to be right under the nose of the illustrious minister, where an exceptionally loud and forceful heckler is directing at him his best, most eloquent credits; 'bastard', 'bollocks', 'fucker', 'traitor' and 'hangman' will convey the general tenor of his remarks. Promptly, he is set upon and is about to be lynched when MacEntee, pausing briefly in his more literate discourse, calls upon his loyal followers to stop.

'That man is an idiot', he says. 'Leave him alone.' Not, perhaps, the most apocalyptic or earth-shaking of utterances, yet such is the power, such is the sense of command he puts into it, that the flying fists and flailing arms drop and the fighting stops at once; and the heckler is left with his hands hanging, wondering what miracle has set him free. It is an early lesson in how MacEntee can use his considerable powers of oratory, first to incite, then to quell an unruly opposition.

That election of 1945 sees him back in power, this time as Minister for Local Government and Public Health. It is a period in which major legislative advances are made to provide a framework for better health and social welfare services, an area which in some respects has not changed much since the days of the workhouse-ward. MacEntee himself, a conservative northerner, had earlier made his mark as Minister for Finance by withstanding all pressures for state-financed welfare schemes. Now, suddenly, he is the pathfinder for radical new changes in the public life.

At that time a family could be plunged into utter destitution when the bread-winner fell ill or died; the rampant plague of tuberculosis could and did wipe out whole households. Against the appalling rate of infant and maternal mortality there was no defence, apart from the work of the religious orders—in recent times either much berated or totally forgotten—and a few philanthropic agencies like the Jubilee and Lady Dudley nursing organisations.

It was a situation which would have a very personal

meaning for me: just two years before that 1945 election, my own father had been forced to give up work due to what a fool of a dispensary doctor diagnosed as bronchitis when even I, as a child, could see it was a great deal worse. And when a short time later he died of TB, our family income rose to twenty-five shillings a week—from the fifteen shillings National Health Insurance it had been during the months of his illness!

In the opening chapter of this book, I give credit to Dr Noel Browne for that first major onslaught on TB. But it was MacEntee's initiatives in setting up the separate Departments of Health and Social Welfare, and the new health and welfare schemes they envisaged, that laid the groundwork for this new approach to two crucial aspects of public life.

The dapper but irascible man standing on the platform on Patrick Street in Cork on that pre-election night in 1945 is the antithesis of the courteous, diffident, affable man with whom I will come in contact close on twenty years later. By then he is over 70 but the same irascible tendency will sometimes come flaming out—a capacity to create dissension where there is none; to make enemies out of people who might be friends; and to draw the fire of people who are doing little more than trying to be helpful in putting forward good ideas.

During a Dublin Corporation bin men's strike for a small increase in pay in the late 1950s, with the streets turning into refuse dumps and the decaying waste rapidly becoming a health hazard, MacEntee—talking over the head of the young Minister for Local Government, Neil Blaney, in whose area of responsibility it properly was—announces with characteristic northern bluntness that 'there will be no increase, large or small'. One might wonder what Lemass, then Taoiseach, thought of that, a man much in favour with the trade unions for his conciliatory skills.

Once, during the Report Stage in the Senate of a Bill on which I did the spadework, an Opposition senator had put down some amendments which, arguably, would have improved it; but whatever animus there was between them (at this remove, I find it hard to remember. Could it have been that he was the nominee of the Irish Medical Organisation, a *bête noire* of MacEntee's at that time?) he is quite determined not to accept them; and not alone not accept, but do so in his best, most acerbic style. Most of what he had to say had little to do with the amendments themselves (again, is my memory astray in thinking that at one point the slaughter of the calves during the Economic War got into the frame?). In any case, what should have been over in five minutes, was still going strong an hour later, with the unfortunate Leader of the House, Tommy Mullins, a former secretary of Fianna Fáil and hence, in part at least, beholden to his lord and master, afraid to open his mouth because, in all probability, if he did, his lord and master would have stalked out!

For good measure, on the way out from that session, the private secretary to the minister next in line to go in takes me aside and asks me angrily why I had told him that we would be out of there in five minutes—leaving him and his minister hanging about for over an hour. A taciturn and rather sullen customer his minister looked too—it was his first outing in the Senate that day. All anyone knew about him was that he was the son-in-law of the then Taoiseach; his name, Charles Haughey.

But on that same occasion I got to see another side of Seán MacEntee, the courteous, gentlemanly side. This was when he accepted, without debate, the amendments put down by Fine Gael Senator Jim Dooge. Dooge, an engineering academic and a most conscientious man, had taken good care to research his amendments, including the wholly sensible but largely unheard-of process of consulting with the administration in advance as to their usefulness. On the way into the Senate chamber, MacEntee makes a comment to me which shows how wrong the popular perception of him is as an unremitting Fine Gael bear-baiter.

'Senator Dooge is not only a scholar,' he says, 'he is also a very intelligent legislator. We are rapidly coming to the point where everything put down by him is proving to be acceptable.'

My civil service mentor in those years was Brendan Hensey, later to become departmental secretary and a good friend. He was an incisive, straight-talking man, much respected for his comprehensive knowledge of the health scene; his definitive commentary *The Health Services of Ireland* earned him a doctorate from UCD. About his mercurial minister he would say that, if he had not been a politician, he would have made a very good civil servant—some tribute from a man who held the trade in such high regard.

At the age MacEntee was when he came to Health, we all thought that it was he himself who had chosen it as a quiet backwater, where he could live out the rest of his working life in semi-retirement. How wrong we were! As he got older, he became more energetic, especially on the legislative side. He was constantly responding to innovative demands to regulate aspects of the health services—dentists, nurses, pharmacists, opticians—which meant that those of us involved with legislation were constantly in and out of

Leinster House. In the last six months of my time there before leaving for RTÉ, he would put no fewer than five Bills through the Houses, an impressive record for any minister and unprecedented for a man then well into his seventies.

On two of those Bills, one dealing with nursing homes, the other with poisons, Brendan Hensey had left it to me to do the preparatory work—Second Reading speeches, Committee and Report Stage briefs, and all the usual back-up correspondence and negotiation such legislation entails. But everything I did had the benefit of being checked and vetted by him. He, however, took sole responsibility for the other three, doing all the administrative work, the checking and vetting himself. Being the exacting man he was, with a well-earned reputation for accuracy and clarity of mind, no one doubted but that he would get everything right. But even Homer nods!

This day, after Minister MacEntee—incidentally, he is always 'Tánaiste' to us, never 'Minister'—has polished off the Report Stage of the Poisons Bill I am working on, he decides to take the Second Reading of a simple Medical Practitioners Bill, one of Brendan's babies. I take myself off to the public gallery until they have finished and he and I can go back to the Custom House together. This will not take long: the Bill sets out to make a small amendment to an earlier Act to allow foreign graduates to do an internship year in Ireland.

The minister delivers his short speech, sits down and waits for what we all assume will be an equally short one from the Opposition. No one is prepared for the bombshell that is about to be dropped. This is delivered by the flamboyant James Dillon who, for some reason which I cannot now recall, is standing in for the shadow Health Minister, Tom

O'Higgins.

How, Dillon demands in his best oratorical style, can the minister refer to this 'thing' as a Bill? As far as he can see, it is nothing but a sheet of green paper. It purports to amend subsection (2) of section 2 of the earlier Act; if the Tánaiste and Minister for Health will take the trouble to look, he will find that there is no subsection (2) in it!

From the gallery above, I can see MacEntee lean across the gangway to where Brendan is sitting in the civil servants' bull-pen; suddenly, out of their whispered conversation, there comes an audible and agitated sound which is certainly not the sound of music! I never feel so sorry for anyone as I do for Brendan Hensey then—a fine man who has never made a mistake in his life. James Dillon, on the far side, sees what is happening and hastens to pour oil on troubled waters. The error, he says, has the virtue of proving one thing: even under Seán MacEntee, there is still some humanity left in the Department of Health! At my own safe remove in the gallery above, I begin to thank my stars that in everything I do I have Brendan to back-stop me; while he, being the thorough person he is, has only himself. Maybe, after all, there is a providence that protects the innocent!

Following the enactment of that Poisons Bill I had worked on, a new council is set up of which I become secretary. The chairman is Desmond O'Malley, a Limerick solicitor, brother of Minister Donogh and father of young Des—then a law student in UCD, with a shock of black hair and a penchant for turning up (I imagine for the goodies his Dad will dispense!) in the Hibernian Hotel on Dawson Street on the last Friday of every month, where I am treated to a fine lunch prior to our council meeting. Among the more effective members are Professor Dick Timoney, to whom the standing of pharmacy as a profession in Ireland owes a great deal, and Professor Maurice Hickey, State Pathologist, a delightful man who, with the lightest touch, will tell the most macabre tales out of school about some 'murders most foul' on which he has been called in. In due course, this council gets itself loaded with the task of adjudicating on the question of the alcohol level in the blood for drink-driving. The figure eventually worked out is based largely on standard European figures at the time—somewhat less, as I remember, than what it is in Ireland even now. In effect, this would mean that not much more that a single pint would exceed it—an edict which, if implemented, would have created such a furore among the free-wheeling drinkers of Erin that it could bring the government down! In the memorandum for government which I put together and which MacEntee in due course signs, the case is cogently argued and the draconian conclusion reached.

Shortly after the government meeting at which it was discussed, I get this phone call from someone who was in on the proceedings and who knew of my involvement with it. It was to say that the Minister for Justice who would be piloting the legislation through the Houses, including the draconian drink figure, had at some stage left his copy of the memorandum in a place where he could see it; and there, on the margin, against the concluding sentence with the one pint drink limit, were the scribbled words: 'Bullshit—and the dope who wrote it knows it!' For yet a second time in my life, I was to be at the cutting edge of its author, Charles Haughey. And many years later, after I have come to know him and recall the incident, his response is that he was certainly right—but graciously concedes that I might have improved a bit since!

It was when I started to write in Irish in the late Fifties and early Sixties that I came into personal contact with the MacEntees, perhaps more especially Margaret Browne, Seán's wife, who had been a lecturer in Irish in UCD and whose daughter, Máire Mhac an tSaoi, a well-known poet, would frequently be published in the monthly *Comhar*, for which I also did regular pieces. At this time, MacEntee would run his more important receptions at the Department of Foreign Affairs (Iveagh House), where Máire was on the diplomatic staff—though that had nothing to do with his being there. Some of us civil servants from Health would be drafted in as glorified lackeys to meet the guests as they arrived and bring them upstairs to where he and his wife would be waiting to receive them. The reception over, they would invite us to join them and their close personal friends for a drink in an ante-room.

'Will 'oo have a drink with us, Paddy?' she enquires one night of the then Minister for Agriculture, Cavan man Paddy Smith. He is affable and florid like herself—she is fondly known as 'Meaig Mór' in their holiday hide-out in Dún Chaoin.

'Indeed and indeed, I will, Margaret,' comes his broad northern response as he takes her by the arm and they go in. 'As the old saying has it, 'twas the drink that brought us down.'

This was the generation of great republican-minded people who had fought for, and won us, our independence. When the MacEntees married at the height of the Troubles, both were 'on the run'; many of the freedom fighters of that time, Michael Collins and Austin Stack among them, were guests at their wedding. She had come from a strongly national-minded family in Tipperary and, like her husband, had been in the GPO in 1916. Three of her brothers were notable churchmen, one a Curia Cardinal in Rome, another, Monsignor Pádraig de Brún, a classical scholar and President of UCG, the third, the modest pastor of Ballymore Eustace, who in his spare time wrote a fine book, *The Big Sycamore*.

Monsignor de Brún was a particularly big influence. Máire would later attribute her superb Kerry Irish to the summers she had spent in that cottage of his above Dún Chaoin. Her four collections, *Margadh na Saoire* (1957), *Codladh an Ghaiscígh* (1973), *An Cion go dtí Seo* (1987) and *Shoa agus Dánta Eile* (1999) are, for my money, among the best things written in Irish in the twentieth century. In his early days Seán MacEntee had been something of a poet himself, with one volume to his credit, *The Poems of John Francis MacEntee*—strongly patriotic stuff, inspired by the events of that sacrificial time. He never really got to grips with the Irish language at all—how could he in the Belfast where he grew up? But the language was a goodly part of the reason why both he and his 'Meaig Mór' loved Dún Chaoin; though, tragically, one night when I was in my usual lackey role at one of their official functions, having just come back from there, I began to enthuse about the place and its people when Margaret, with very evident pathos, shook her great florid head and sighed: 'Tá na blianta caite, Liam. Ní dóigh liom go bhfeicfimid Dún Chaoin go deo arís!'

The family attachment to the language would come to a strange flowering one misty morning a few summers later when the local co-operative, Comharchumann Chorca Dhuibhne, was running a seminar, one of the events at which was a talk by Máire Mhac an tSaoi on aspects of Gaelic literature. It was held in the capacious but draughty Halla na Muirí near the village of Ballyferriter. Whatever about the draughts, its capaciousness was quite unnecessary. For just seven people turned up: Máire's two young nephews, the

Biggar boys, Síle Humphreys, veteran of the War of Independence celebrated in Ernie O'Malley's fine book *The Singing Flame*, and her two grandsons, and my wife and I—a sparse if appreciative audience, at least three of whom might be just about old enough to appreciate anything at all! If I use the phrase, 'pearls before swine', it is not to denigrate our collective intelligence, but to emphasise that pearls were indeed what were about to be cast before us. For the talk to which we were treated would be fit matter for a doctoral thesis. With her encyclopaedic knowledge of her subject, the thrust and clarity of her delivery, above all, her passion to communicate the depth and richness of the native literary seam, I do not think I have ever heard a scholarly talk to equal it. A diplomat she was by profession, a poet by vocation, a wife and mother later on; in all those roles I am sure she excelled. But, on that morning in a windswept hall in west Kerry, I got the distinct feeling that she had missed her one real vocation, teaching. It is surely a commentary on Irish academia that so fine a teaching talent was never on the permanent academic staff of any of our universities.

'Teacher', on the other hand, was not a word his contemporaries would ever have used about her father. Yet, in my limited experience, at his best that is what he was, patient, keen to clarify when things were not clear, ready to supply from his prodigious memory accurate footnotes on anything requiring elucidation. One quirky little tale will help to illustrate this: the Hospitals Trust fund, a main source in its time for hospitals' building and maintenance, was being endangered by the threatened introduction of a new lottery to compete with the Sweepstakes, which were the fund's financial base. So he sets about preparing this Bill, the effect of which will be to exclude other lotteries from the range of what he describes as 'eleemosynary' activities. The Bill, as it happens, never sees the light of day; but you, good reader, must wonder now, as I did then, what this strange word might mean. (For what it's worth—how can you have lived your life without knowing?—it means a dependence on charity for existence or, in straight terms, charitable.) Years later, when I have long gone from the civil service, I meet him in the hospitality suite in RTÉ, where he is having a post-programme drink with some other participants in a 'Today Tonight' programme. The subject for discussion on the programme had been the setting up of a new semi-state board; and a question occurs to me as we chat: why could this not be done by the simple process of setting it up as a company under company law, rather than go through the time-consuming and possibly acrimonious process of putting a Bill through the Houses of the Oireachtas?

Ever the teacher, MacEntee proceeds to explain. Where it is an agreed matter of public policy—the Mass Radiography Association in combating TB, the Blood Transfusion Association for the supply of blood, St Luke's Hospital for the treatment of cancer—there is no policy issue at stake; in such cases, company law is the route to take; but where there are other sides to the argument—as, for instance, had been the case with the Voluntary Health Insurance Board—then it should be put through the process of parliamentary debate, so that all possible aspects of it can be tested and teased out. Having said all this, he stops.

'Why are you asking me this, Liam?' he says. 'You know the answer to that question very well yourself?'

'If I do,' I say light-heartedly, 'it is you who taught me.'

Then, in the slight stammer he affects before coming in for the kill, he adds: 'I n...n...never taught you anything.'

'Indeed you did,' I say. We are into light banter now and the others are enjoying it. 'You taught me the meaning of the word "eleemosynary".'

'Ah yes,' he says, without a second's hesitation. 'That was the time we were doing the Lotteries legislation.'

Speak for yourself, dear reader, but for me, if I can remember when I am 80 a particular time when I used a particular word, then lump me with those elephants who never forget!

Some of the above reminiscences were recorded in a radio interview I did some time later with the late John Skehan as part of an obituary programme he was preparing against what was widely thought to be the imminent demise of Seán MacEntee. He is well into his 80s by then, with most of his contemporaries already dead. But he does not die, neither then, nor for most of a decade later. When eventually that does happen, John rings me again, this time to ask if I can suggest someone who would have known him in his last years in office. The name I give him is Joe Robins, his former private secretary. Joe would tell him about the traumas of those years, including the trauma of daughter Máire being found in Africa with Conor Cruise O'Brien when the Katanga conflict broke out. I cannot say if John Skehan ever spoke to Joe; what I do know is that he had to remind me that I had already done an interview with him myself about the Custom House years, an interview which I had clean forgotten—so much for *this* particular elephant's memory! But, he asks me, if there's anything I would like to add to what I had said in that interview ten years before. It so happens that there was: it was about the very last conversation I had with Seán MacEntee, one that took place on the morning of the funeral of Fianna Fáil veteran and founder-member, Joe Groome. Groome's Hotel, opposite Dublin's Gate Theatre, was a favourite watering-hole for politicians, performers and the general public—in that order: public in the outer bar, actors/performers in the next, and politicians—including some illustrious ministerial ones—in the inner sanctum beyond.

Many of that motley crew of 'maithe agus mór-uaisle' turn up at the old man's funeral; and, in the crowd, now close on 90 years old but still quite chipper in himself, is his old friend and comrade-in-arms, Seán MacEntee. Coming down the steps of the Pro Cathedral, I ask him if he will be going on with the funeral to Glasnevin. No, he says, he has got too old for that, and will head back home. Home is on Trimleston Avenue, just off the Merrion Road, and hence quite near RTÉ. Since that is where I am headed, rather than have him stand around waiting for a taxi, I drive him out.

Old in years he may be, but old in other ways he is not. When, in some casual way the subject of my own background comes up, I tell him about my Dublin Fusiliers father, who had come through the Boer War and the Great War and who, when he had a few drinks in, would say about the Rising of 1916 that he had 'often seen more shootin'' done before me breakfast!' When I further tell him that from hearing about my father's time in the Boer War, the names of Kruger, Smuts, Cronje and Botha were more familiar to me as a boy than the names of de Valera or Michael Collins, he is quite visibly astonished. How, from such a background, he asks, do I come to have such an obvious concern for the Irish language and Irish culture, something which, he says, comes across very clearly on radio and television?

We are into a most absorbing conversation now. The Christian Brothers are mentioned, as is the influence of

Daniel Corkery in UCC and, later, the songs and music programmes on the old Radio Éireann run by people like Seán Óg Ó Tuama and Seán Ó Riada. Being perhaps a smarter politician than I think I am—or, perhaps more truthfully, wanting to lift an old man's heart—the quality of his own daughter's writing in Irish gets honourable mention. It is but a short step from here to his own progress in the freedom struggle; and an even shorter one to the Treaty of 1921, when the whole idealistic thrust underlying that struggle became soured in the bitter recriminations of the Civil War.

How, I ask him, could such deeply patriotic people as you were have fought and killed each other, when the desired goal was very nearly in sight; when the nation's resources which you then had to hand could have been used to build up a new Ireland to the point where the people up north might look across the border and say, 'They're making such a good fist of things down there, maybe we could look again at the idea of joining them?'

Upon reflection, I have to say that I must have consumed a fair amount of the good man's whiskey to have come out with such treasonable talk. For—there is no other word for it—I see now that it was pure Michael Collins 'stepping-stone' stuff, the very essence of the pro-treaty case, though his name was never mentioned; nor indeed, to be truthful, had it at all crossed my mind.

Suddenly, he is up and away. For a moment, I think he has taken ill; then, more ominously, that I have offended him and he is about to throw me out. Neither happens. Instead, I hear him running up the stairs—yes, running, at close on 90 years old! A moment later, he is back down and has a volume of the *Treaty Debates* in his hand.

'There, read that', he says, striking it open at the page he wants and hands it to me. It is a speech by a member of the first Dáil—can it have been himself or his revered Dev?—saying the very thing I had been saying just then.

'So you see,' he firmly reminds me, 'you are not the first person to have had ideas like that. But, what you and young [!] people like you will never understand is that there was a great deal more at stake at that time than the bread-and-butter things which that argument is all about—and which seem to be the only things that matter to anyone now!'

A whole generation has grown up since Seán MacEntee said that, and several generations have come and gone since these issues of 1921/22 were to the fore. But the more substantial issues of that time—certainly the ones that northerner, Seán MacEntee, would have cared about—are still there. Following that troubled time, the North did indeed become what MacEntee said it would become, 'England's fortress in Ireland, a fortress as impregnable as Gibraltar'. And while the Celtic Tiger of our time may have ushered in better times down south—to say nothing of the promising arrangements made under the Good Friday Agreement—there is as yet little sign of that 'unity of hearts and minds' around 'the dreary spires of Fermanagh and Tyrone'. Following the execution of Roger Casement in 1916, poet John Francis MacEntee would write:

> . . . nor shall the proud sword know its sheath
> Till they fulfil the task that he essayed,
> And freedom's name to free-born sons bequeath.

If that ideal was not achieved in his time, a sufficient measure of it *was* achieved for a sovereign Ireland to 'take her place among the nations of the earth'. 'The Re-integration of the National Territory' was the title of a file being put together at his instigation in the Department of Health during my time there; it is no doubt gathering dust now in some forgotten corner of Gandon's Custom House. Aspirational it undoubtedly was, but it did have the makings of some form of cross-border co-operation in selected areas of public life, including health, which is a main plank in the arrangements under the Good Friday Agreement now. In this respect Seán MacEntee was in the same visionary mould as John Hume and Séamus Mallon of these times; even in their way the once poles apart but rapidly converging Gerry Adams/Martin McGuinness axis of Sinn Féin and the David Ervine/Billy Hutchinson axis of the Progressive Unionist Party. With luck and a little patience, some new young hopefuls may yet come along to carry the reintegration process to a conclusion.

All that is for the commentators and historians. For me, what remains is the memory of a gracious old man with whom I was privileged to have a brief but rewarding association. Before leaving him that day of Joe Groome's funeral, fascinated as I was by his discourse, I suggested to him that he do a self-portrait documentary-type programme with me for radio or television—an idea which he rejected out of hand.

'Having talked with you here now for the past few hours,' he says, 'I feel so exhausted that all I'm fit for is the bed!'

Well, at close on 90, who wouldn't? Maybe it was as well. What he had to say he had said—too bitterly and too often, some detractors in his own time would surely add! The only thing of substance that might have remained for him to say—the ultimate achievement of that Irish unity so dear to him—would certainly not be said in his lifetime. If, in recent years, it has come a shade closer, it is in no small measure due to the persistence and steadfastness of Seán MacEntee and of the men and women of his time.

What might stand for all of them is Hamlet's testament to his dead father: 'He was a man, take him for all in all, I shall not look upon his like again.' Or, in the idiom of An tOileánach of An Blascaod Mór, a part of the country he came to love, though far from his native Belfast home: 'Ní bheidh a leithéid arís ann.'

Larger Than Life

BISHOP ÉAMONN CASEY

'There's a wonderful Irish priest working over in Slough. When you get home to Ireland, hire a film crew and come back here and make a programme with him.'

This remark was made to me in London in May 1964. I was at the BBC Training Centre in Lime Grove near Beggars' Bush doing a television-producer course before taking up a job as editor of Irish language programmes in RTÉ. Among the instructors there were some who became well-known names in the years to come: David Frost, David Attenborough, Don Baverstock, Huw Weldon, Alisdair Milne. But it was none of those who told me about this 'wonderful Irish priest working over in Slough' but a preacher, a lecturer, a Franciscan priest who was then Catholic Religious Adviser to the BBC, and later to the Vatican on media affairs. His name was Agnellus Andrew.

'If the Irish hierarchy have any sense,' he went on, 'they'll get this fellow back as quick as they can and give him a big job in Ireland.'

The 'fellow' was Éamonn Casey. As it happens, I never get to see him during his time in Slough, though I did get to see some other Irish priests, who were part of the chaplaincy scheme to the emigrant Irish in Britain in those years. In the Irish Centre in Camden Town, run largely by them, their function was to pick up every waif and stray who fetched up on England's sweet shore, and help them find digs, jobs, friends and relations, and anything else they might need; this also included non-public house entertainments, especially over the weekend nights when their fine hall would serve as a springboard for many a big name in the entertainment world—Val Doonican, Brendan Shine, Dave Allen, the Fureys, the Wolfe Tones.

This Father Casey of Slough seemed to have done some of that too, but he did one thing more. This was in the realm of finding homes for people, a widespread and burning concern for newly-weds and young families in Britain right then. He had become involved with the Housing Aid Society, a non-sectarian co-operative in whose ranks were to be found members of all religions and none, including some who were out and out communists. Dare the word be spoken in those post-Cuban missile crisis Cold War years! Father Casey would say, as had the charismatic Pope John XXIII before him, that he had no problem working with communists or anyone else either for that matter, provided they were working to the same agenda as he was: the simple, fundamental rule of 'love thy neighbour'—by serving him.

Those early Sixties were a time when the hierarchy back home were still locked to a traditional past. It had been little more than a decade since 'the belt of a crozier' had levelled Noel Browne and made his well-intentioned Mother and Child Scheme look as if it had been spawned by the devil. A largely docile and devotional laity still adhered to the strict tenets of whatever their bishops and priests laid down. The role of the Church, though overtly limited to religious and moral affairs, extended well beyond those into the highways and byways of ordinary secular life. The idea of an Irish priest becoming involved with communists, even in so worthy a cause as finding homes for the homeless, was a sacrilege. Yet also, and to be fair to them—who nowadays is?—it was this same hierarchy which, in the first place, had devised that Irish chaplaincy scheme which was doing such splendid work among Irish emigrants in Britain. So it is not beyond the bounds of possibility that some of them at least must have seen Casey's work in Slough and wondered what effect it might have if he were to be brought back to Ireland. Here indeed would be something new in Irish ecclesiastical life: an innovator, a pathfinder, an entrepreneur, a breaker of moulds and a maker of new ones—a man who would, like the reigning Irish-American icon of that time, John F. Kennedy, 'dare dream dreams and ask—why not?'

So when it was announced that he was to become Bishop of Kerry, the few who knew him from his London years knew that fireworks could be expected. In short order, he had activity groups and committees springing up all around him, with people with the same electric charge attached to them as he had himself in seeing to it that things got done— among them Frank Lewis, a PR man, and Father (now Archbishop) Dermot Clifford, a sociologist by profession and a man who knew, as Éamonn Casey himself did, what a waste of time it was to be preaching religion to people who hadn't a job or enough to eat or a roof over their heads. Crucial to all this was the growing importance of the young and their relevance to the development of a new emphasis upon the restoration of local, regional and national self-confidence. Jobs were crucial to it, the economy central to a cultural and entertainment revival. 'Kerry for Youth' schemes were launched to create an active new awareness. In a word, a whole new dynamic began to build up around him, in which the tardiness and inertia of the past was replaced by a forward-looking sense of progress and optimism. This was religion in its practical sense, caring for the body of the faithful, so that they might have a soul with which to say thanks when the body's needs were met.

Nowhere was this more evident than in cultural activity, where every local venture which sought the new bishop's support got it in full measure. It was through one such venture that I eventually met the 'wonderful Irish priest over in Slough'—the Siamsa group in Tralee. To begin with, this was nothing more than what many towns in Ireland had at the time: a church choir and an Irish dancing school. But, with the arrival in Tralee of a gifted choirmaster, Father Pat Aherne, it soon developed into what would become the finely choreographed folk performances now known under the title of 'Siamsa Tíre'.

How the Siamsa group first came to my attention is a story in itself. I had just come back to RTÉ from that BBC producer course and among my early programme ideas was one to help people come to an understanding of the great songs in Irish which, without a knowledge of the language, would be wellnigh impossible. Was there a way, I asked myself, in which their story could be visually told, a kind of mime of the story line which would make the meaning clear? Sometimes you work at things for ever and nothing happens; other times they fall into your lap. This night, on a reel of grotty old film cued into a 'Tangents' programme run by Frank Hall, I see this group dancing to the song 'Casadh an tSúgáin' (The twisting of the straw rope). It tells the story of a young fellow who comes a-courting the daughter of the local big-wig who doesn't want him. So the girl's mother gets him to twist a straw rope with her across the length of the floor until at last she has him out the door. Once out, she slams the door in his face and won't let him back in. On this clip of film the story is told by the mime—music, song, dance—all going together to make an instantly intelligible scene. It is in fact 'Riverdance' three decades before its time.

There and then, I seek out the man who made the film, Pádraig Kennelly—'a fierce hoor of a Kerryman', he tells me when we first meet! He in turn refers me to the priest-organiser, Pat Aherne, then a new curate in St John's, Tralee. Pat had done a B.Mus. with Seán Ó Riada in UCC and was consumed with the same idea that I had—to communicate the sense of the great songs in Irish to people who do not know the language. So I put the proposition to him that he create a set of sequences similar to what he has done with 'Casadh an tSúgáin', which I will then build into the series I am planning. Shortly afterwards, it emerges as 'Aililiú'. Seán Ó Riada's Ceoltóirí Chualann do some of the programmes, as do Cabaret Gael Linn, and a brightly costumed group from away off in the Connemara Gaeltacht, Cabaret Chárna. But Pat Aherne's Siamsa is the sheet anchor which holds the whole series together.

Some short time after that Pat rings me to say that Bishop Casey and a few friends would like me to join them, with a view to launching a new Siamsa management group. We meet in the Gresham in Dublin. There are five of us: Bishop Éamonn, Father Pat, Dr Séamus Wilmot, Chairman of the Abbey, Brendan O'Regan of the Shannon Free Airport Development Company, and myself. Brendan O'Regan's entrepreneurial skills come into play at once; a family hotelier by profession, he was the one who had pioneered the whole notion of duty-free shops; he had been a prime mover in the development of Shannon Airport and the setting up of Shannon town—the first Irish town to be founded in the second millennium—drawing its population and strength from his personal brain child, SFADCO. Finally, when things got out of hand in the North, he was the one who had dreamed up the idea of 'Co-operation North', a pathfinder in the creation of practical north–south relations.

Within minutes, Brendan has jotted down the headings for a new management company, of which Séamus Wilmot will later become chairman. Out there on the wings like a protecting spirit is Bishop Éamonn, a back-up and a support to which Pat Aherne's singers and dancers warmly respond. But part of their problem in those early years is that they have no permanent home; the stop-gap is a disused and crumbling old cinema in Tralee. So architect Paddy O'Sullivan is commissioned to design a brand new theatre, all mod con, tailored to the needs of the choral, mime and dance ensemble that Siamsa is. When the estimated cost is announced (half a million or more—small money now but not thirty-odd years ago), people fall under the table with the shock. Not so Éamonn Casey. He has faced such shocks before with the Housing Aid Society in London and got round them because the will was there. If he has anything to do with it, it will be there now too.

'We have a magnificent programme to show them in this theatre,' he tells us. 'That is all we need to sell the idea. Convince our benefactors of that, and the money will come.' Ways and means of raising it are discussed: sales of work, car and holiday raffles, house-to-house collections, bob-a-jobs—all the usual boring routines followed by good folk in pursuit of good causes. Meanwhile, Éamonn sits there silent, sucking his pipe.

'All that is fine,' he says, 'and may come to something in a century or two. We need this theatre now. There is only one way to collect money like that. Go directly to the people who have it and ask them for it.'

'Has his lordship any idea who those people might be?' chairman Wilmot asks.

'Of course I have. We all have. We all know people and companies who will be only too willing to sponsor an enterprise like Siamsa, once it's properly explained to them. But you must take time to do it. You must sit down with them and tell them the point and purpose of it. If necessary, invite them along to see the show, to meet the people involved and see for themselves the commitment that's there. And you don't confine yourself to Ireland. Ten big sponsors giving fifty thousand each will do it, from the US, Britain and here. But we must give it our time.'

The rest of us look at each other in consternation. Who might those ten gold-mine sponsors be? Who will do the talking with them? We are all busy men and women—where will we find the time? Éamonn, used to such nullity from his years in Slough, judges our mood and knows that some prodding may be needed. Do we not know that faith can move mountains?

'If I could spring myself loose for long enough,' he tells us, 'I would do it myself in a month.' It so happens that on the board with us by then is the courteous and diffident Church of Ireland Bishop of Meath (later Archbishop of Dublin) Dónall Caird. Dónall sits there, as do the rest of us, spellbound by such self-confidence. I can see him contrasting the meagre takings from his diminishing parishes with this apparently effortless barnstorming. Séamus Wilmot, a scholar in his own right but, more to the point, an astute Kerryman, sits there ruminatively, biting on the stem of his short pipe.

'Through the Chair,' Bishop Dónall asks, 'do I understand his lordship to say that he could collect half a million pounds in a month?'

Astute and scholarly the Kerry chairman may be, a man too with a proper respect for the Church, its cloth and the clerical proprieties; but he knows well when a bombshell lands in front of him and responds promptly in his true and native tongue:

'Lord Chrisht Almighty,' he says, 'isn't that what he has just said—my lord!'

Anyway, the money is raised and after an interim period in the refurbished Regal Cinema, the architect's dream comes true. The Siamsa Tíre Theatre is there today in the centre of Tralee as a splendid monument to the tenacity of the founding fathers; as are the Siamsa folk houses in Finuge near Listowel and Carraig near Ballyferriter—focal points for the native cultural life of those outlying regions.

Éamonn's presence at the Siamsa meetings always guaranteed a lively time. It was especially delightful to watch himself and Brendan O'Regan in action together, both pathfinders in their way but so very different in their approach: Éamonn ebullient, outspoken, outgoing, whether in laughter or confrontation—the whole place goes quiet when he speaks; Brendan, taciturn, measured, seeing before anyone else the compromises that must be made to make things work. His ability to grasp and shape an idea so as to make it workable within the resources available is indeed remarkable; it is surely what Seán Lemass, as Minister for Industry and Commerce, had seen long years before when he gave him a formative role in the Shannon development idea. In his hesitant, thoughtful way, he would remind me again and again of that image of visionary leadership in Yeats's great poem 'The Long-Legged Fly':

That civilisation may not sink,
Its great battle lost,
Quiet the dog, tether the pony
To a distant post;
Our master Caesar is in the tent
Where the maps are spread,
His eyes fixed upon nothing,
A hand under his head.
Like a long-legged fly upon the stream
His mind moves upon silence.

The general public soon got to know Éamonn Casey from his appearances on television. The first programme he did with me was a talk-show called 'Gairm'—it means a calling or vocation. This was shot on Saturday mornings in a corner of the 'Late Late' set. His Irish was just about up to it, though with the help of Antoin Ó Sé from Ballyferriter—just back from Chicago and, like Éamonn, deeply committed to the development of local communities (in his case, it was the dynamic West Kerry Co-op., Comharchumann Chorca Dhuibhne)—everything went fine. When it was all over, we repaired to the hospitality suite for a drink. It was early December and that night there would be a big get-together in Tralee to celebrate some recent Kerry success. The following morning, the bishop would be in Clochán under Mount Brandon to say a special Mass to celebrate the village's winning of the Glór na Gael prize. Tom O'Donnell, affable Fine Gael Minister for the Gaeltacht, would also be there, as would all my old friends from Ballyferriter. Would I not come along to be with them? Éamonn would drive me, put me up, look after everything. No sooner said than done. Promptly, I am in the back seat of the Mercedes with Antoin

Ó Sé and we are on our way to the Kingdom.

Éamonn's typist-secretary, Patricia Gilbride, picks us up at the Gresham and drives as far as the Naas Road; there, he himself takes over and she goes to the passenger seat. It is dark now but, with the press of a button, she flicks on the overhead light and a lap-top desk opens in front of her. From then, for fully two hours till we get to Nenagh, there is a flood of cards, letters, phone messages which she reads aloud to him and to which he dictates replies. They are not just from Ireland; they are from all over the world. Each has a personal message or request; each gets an immediate response. Never in any office I have ever been in have I seen such sustained intensity. How can he keep his mind on the driving, I ask myself, while all this is going on? But he does, and meticulously too. He certainly needs a good car under him, and an even better and steadier set of nerves.

We make our first stop at the roadside hotel in Nenagh. There is a drink—for Éamonn it is a single whiskey and water. Then, it is back to the car, where Patricia again takes the wheel and he goes to the passenger seat where he promptly falls asleep. This lasts the twenty minutes to Birdhill, where they change places again. From there, it is the same routine the whole way to Killarney. I begin to see what Father Agnellus Andrew at the BBC meant that day some years before when he spoke about a 'wonderful Irish priest over in Slough'.

Nor is that the end of it. In his house in Killarney—when did the Church give up that grandiose and silly notion of calling those places 'palaces'?—the moment he arrives, there is a bevy of priest-secretaries in across the scene, each with his own pressing business and urgent agenda. I cannot now recall if his imperturbable personal secretary, Dermot Clifford, was there; but he is surely the one who will have to pick up the pieces the following Monday morning to see that everything discussed that night is done.

And then we are off again, this time to a get-together in a hall in Tralee for another Kingdom event. All the 'maithe agus mór-uaisle' of Kerry are there, the dances are danced, and Éamonn sings 'Oh, the days of them'. By now, it is near midnight and he has been going since six in the morning. But we still have a way to go. So it's back into the car and off out another thirty miles to his home above Inch Strand, a heavenly place in the daylight, but not at midnight when the eyes are dropping out of your head with sleep.

'Now that we're safely home,' he tells me, 'we'll have a drink. But, first we have a bit of work to do. I'm saying Mass in Irish in the morning and I want it to go right. So we'll just go through it together, then we can sit back and relax.'

The 'sit back and relax' comes half an hour later when the linguistic fine-tuning is done. Soon, the conversation takes an interesting turn—to be precise, to family and sexual matters, and how the Church is dealing with them. Why, I ask, are the priests and preachers always going on about aberrations and deviations, when there is a whole positive side to married life which never gets a mention at all: the openness, the security, the positive side of fidelity? Why are we, the so called faithful, constantly being hectored and lectured about the evils of divorce, separation, abortion, contraception and all the rest, when there is a whole rich territory out there where these things need not be the issue at all; but, rather, how to make the love affairs that become marriages remain love affairs? If that idea could be restored—and how else could it be done but by talking about it?—some shaky marriages might be saved; and some good but boring ones made a great deal better.

Clearly, I must have put away a fair amount of the good

man's Paddy to have got such a load off my chest. His response seemed to be one of curious but bewildered interest. Not for the first or the last time in my life, it occurs to me that this is the kind of talk which only married people can exchange with any degree of credibility. In seminaries, confessionals or elsewhere, do high ecclesiastics ever get to hear it? (All right, be patient, I am aware that Éamonn, a celibate priest, did have some non-celibate experience and I will come to it, but for now, let me continue with this.) For while I have no wish to enter the recurring discussion about a celibate priesthood, it does indeed strike me—and, despite all we have heard since about the covert carry-on of some clerics, it still strikes me—that no amount of priestly or holy learning can ever match the experience of those who have actually lived the life.

Which, in a way, brings me back to square one: that it is the parents—the mothers and fathers who have lived the life—who should be the real teachers in this field, if only some god or man or other instrument of power could be got to unfreeze the unholy silence that seems to surround it and get them to talk openly, before the whole shebang goes up in smoke.

I must not, however, give a wrong impression. The weekend would not be all solemn morality. I have no idea what time it was by the time the above got said; it was certainly well into the small hours when what remained of the bottle of Paddy was finally put away, and we go off to bed to sleep the sleep of the just. For this particular morsel of 'justness', that would usually mean until eight or nine the following morning. But I have no sooner put my head on the pillow than I hear the shower going and someone is singing in there: it is him—and he is already up and on his way. I look at my watch: it is ten to seven and pitch dark. There is a knock on my door and his lordship of Kerry bids me welcome the new-born day!

'Get up when you feel like it,' he says. 'I'll get us a bit of breakfast, then we can be on our way. It'll take us over an hour to get to Brandon.'

In the pearly frost the morning drive by the mountain road from Inch is white and very beautiful, the fuchsia heavy with the night rain and the little lakes on the wayside like the eyes of children opening upon the new day's light. The road is narrow up there, all twists and hairpins; but the black Merc. and its episcopal driver are well able for it. When we get to the main road—if 'main' is not too grandiose a word!—he puts the boot down and away we go until, suddenly, up ahead, a garda car comes in sight. It is headed the same way as we are—out to the Glór na Gael celebration under Mount Brandon beyond. Instantly, he applies the brakes and we follow at a discreet distance.

'There's a thing never to do,' I am counselled, 'that is embarrass the guards. They're only doing a job like the rest of us. Part of it is to see that fellas like me don't cause problems.'

Early as it is, the crowd has already gathered outside the parish church as we arrive. Tom O'Donnell's ministerial car is there but the minister himself is nowhere in sight. Having arrived early, we surmise he has already gone in. The moment the Bishop steps out of the car, he is surrounded by well-wishers on all sides, all keen to shake hands and have a word with the 'great man'—and spend the rest of the week talking about it! Éamonn goes in among them, both hands out to greet them, the picture and epitome of 'Sagart Aroon' in the song. There being no way in this situation that he can carry the long black case which has his bishop's mitre, robes and folded staff, I am given charge of it and told to go ahead into the sacristy and tell them he'll be along in a minute.

It is relevant to say that, at this time I have only just started my front-of-house life in television and my face is not as well known as it will later be. More to the point, Minister O'Donnell has only recently become a minister and is not known to people at all. So as I walk in through the crowd, then up the aisle of the church, I notice that they are all smiling and bowing to me. Is it because of the official-looking case I am carrying? Or is it the official-looking dark overcoat which makes me look as if I might be one of the great man's attendants? But, already, I am near the top; and there, at the end of the pew, is Tom O'Donnell, all alone, with no one taking any notice of him at all. As I come up beside him, one of the lay folk in a cluster up there comes forward to greet me.

'Tá fáilte romhat anseo, a Aire,' he tells me warmly as we shake hands. 'Tá sé an-dheas uait teacht anseo le bheith inár measc.' (You're welcome, Minister. It's very nice of you to come and be with us.) It is the first and, I hope, the last time I will have such greatness thrust upon me!

There would be yet one small fragment of fall-out from that polemical chin-wag in Bishop Éamonn's house in Inch that Saturday night. This happens a while later when I come across a poem—by a J. M Cameron, a poet whose name I have never heard—in *The Times Literary Supplement*, which states the argument against abortion more compellingly than any episcopal or clerical statement I have ever read. So, remembering our conversation that night, I send him a copy, asking him whether it mightn't deserve an airing on radio or television. In a brief reply, he says no, it is too explicit, too tetchy for an Irish audience at that time and might well cause more offence than enlightenment.

So I forget all about it until recently when, by chance, it slips out of a file of papers I happen to be reading. I have to say now that I think he was wrong. For it is indeed a splendid piece of work, dodging none of the issues in that heavily laden minefield. For what it is worth, twenty-one years after I first read it, here it is:

Public Vices, Private Benefits
'Pregnancy goes about frankly and freely, indeed with pride, while coitus hides itself away like a criminal.' Schopenhauer

> In midnight woods, round corners, and in bed
> In former days men took the maidenhead
> Or sluiced the matron. Here's a finer age
> When public copulation's all the rage,
> In common spectacles the two-backed beast
> Tickles the fancy, decorates the feast.

> Then too, the woman who grew ripely round,
> Displayed her shape and firmly trod the ground.
> Was thought a pleasure to the public eye,
> An antidote to human misery,
> An ark of majesty, a house of bread,
> To warm the living and console the dead.

> Now as we watch the climax of the f★★★
> We scratch our doxies or bemoan our luck.
> All think that if by some strange accident
> An egg is waiting as the seed is spent
> The consequence is void—no need to blush,
> For we can poison, macerate or crush
> The frail intruder, lest he block the way
> Of the night's folly or business of the day.

All's relative in this, I hear one cavil,
What comes from the good God, what from the Devil,
Which is the murderer and which the victim,
Which is the gull and which the one who tricked him —
These are large matters for the Commonwealth
To be remitted to the priests of health,
Grave doctors of the law, and fancy preachers
With fancy sentiments and foxy features.

Prince, patron, reader, husband, wife, or friend,
Look to the horrid means, the bitter end.
You kill a foetus as you kill a cold
(For, my dear man, it's less than three months old),
Then throw it out as garbage or (more prudent)
Give it to some investigating student
With buoyant and emancipated mind,
Murderous to save and cruel to be kind.
But recollect before you're quite undone
The life you squander is the life you own.

Éamonn's transfer to Galway seemed to make him more accessible to us programme-makers in RTÉ. Following his installation there—memorable for the great night's singing and entertainment that followed—he would come on to 'Trom Agus Éadrom' whenever we asked him, perhaps most notably on the 'Up for the Final' Eve of All Ireland special of 1980 when Galway won the hurling final for the first time in fifty-seven years. He was a natural for TV—the phrase we used about him was that he 'filled the box'. His instant willingness to come on to my programmes sometimes surprised me, until one day I asked his secretary, Fr Jimmy McLoughlin (now Bishop), about it. His response was highly flattering: 'I asked him that once myself and what he said was: "With Liam I know I won't be blackguarded."'

We come finally to the Annie Murphy affair and Bishop Casey's fall from grace. Let me say at once that I know no more about this than anyone else does, if indeed there is anything more to be known after all the publicity it got at the time. My sole comment is the more general one that, in my view, the thing was wholly predictable. I could not help noticing on the one night I spent in that house in Inch how remote and lovely a place it was. Having once been a parish house but then no longer needed, it was about to be sold off when Éamonn, just back from London and on a round of diocesan properties, saw it and fell for it at once: a place of great tranquillity, far from the hustle and bustle of his thriving office; a place for thought and reflection, with the daily forty-five minute drive to and from Killarney, giving him, as he himself told me, all the time in the world he needed for praying. In a word, a place of perfect peace and isolation—alas, for trysting too for someone in that frame of mind. Let there be no doubt about it, that would have been about the last thing in his mind when he brought an attractive young woman to live under the same roof with him—recovering, too, as she was from a broken marriage and glad of the counsel and companionship of a family priest-friend. But, as any sensible married man would have told him, priest or no priest, celibate or no celibate, as a male man he was playing with fire. 'Tosach seirce síor-shilleadh', says an old Irish phrase: love begins with constant looking. Living in the same house with a young woman, constantly looking at her, where else would his thoughts not sooner or later turn? There was something primevally innocent about the way Éamonn Casey walked into it.

In his novel, *That Uncertain Feeling*, Kingsley Amis has this married university lecturer, just free from one torrid love affair, about to be caught up in another; his wife, a realist and down to earth woman, knows her man and recognises the signs: 'Christ,' she says, 'what's lover-boy getting himself pitched up to now?' She knows well that he'll be in trouble if he stays; so the moment the tell-tale signs begin to show, she asks no questions, just packs their bags and off she hauls him to a job in another place, mysteriously flinging at him her sole caveat: 'He who loveth the danger perisheth therein.'

The pity is that someone close to him wasn't around to say that to Éamonn. The moment he began to see his protégée not as victim, a fellow human being to be helped and counselled, but as a human being in the full flower of womanhood, the scented pollen had already begun to drift. From then on there was but one way for it to go. In this he was no different from the rest of us, weak, susceptible, constantly at risk from a hundred and one temptations in the lovely, everyday world about us.

In his case, priest and bishop that he was, one might have thought that the grace of God might prove stronger than temptation; but the grace of God can be quite intangible betimes, while the sight of a handsome young woman in the room next door to you is not. 'Be not familiar with any woman', says Thomas à Kempis in his *Imitation of Christ*, 'but recommend all good women to God.' But when the 'good woman' is there beside you, day in day out, is it not asking a mite too much of mere flesh and blood to shut her permanently out of sight and mind? Éamonn's sin—if such it be, rather than breaking a man-made Church rule—could be the sin of any of us. And his high moral ground detractors ought to be careful about casting the first stone.

Anyway, it all happened a long time ago and he has suffered grievously for it since. So indeed has the woman, their son too—but they are not the subject of this memoir. The fact that Éamonn lost everything—his office, his good name, the extraordinary charisma he carried about with him through all the London, Kerry and Galway years—all that is surely a source of deep and abiding grief. But he did not lose his life, or his priesthood which, as we know, means so much to him. Is it too much to ask at this late stage that he be restored without delay to the country he loves and the people he served so well? Ireland, the Irish Church, the Irish people owe him that much at least—not a great deal, but it is all that is left. For that small mercy, the 'wonderful Irish priest over in Slough' would surely say, 'Go raibh míle maith agat.'

The Heart, A Lonely Hunter

CYRIL CUSACK

The first time I hear the name Cyril Cusack, it has nothing to do with acting or the theatre at all. This was from a well-known, well-respected sage in Dalkey, one Paddy Darcy, who had been with him in the Druid's Chair in Killiney the night before, when the subject of the Lane pictures came up.

This Darcy was a remarkable man. Older than Cyril and the others in the company that night, he was much admired and looked up to by them all, not least because of his prodigious historical and literary knowledge, but also because, quite contrary to his family background, at the age of 16 he had taken his RIC father's bicycle and revolver and cycled into Dublin to take part in the Rising of 1916. When the 'split' came, he took the republican side, was a close friend of 'hard men' like Ernie O'Malley and Peadar O'Donnell, and was reputed to be the last man on the east coast to hand up his gun. 'Decommission' was not a word that was heard of in those years.

He had held steadfastly to his republican principles ever since, even to the point where he had a service pension which he never cashed, saying it was not for profit or advantage they had done it. Though never 'old' in the usual sense—when well into his seventies he swam regularly at the Rampart below Vico Road, occasionally also at the Forty Foot in

Sandycove; if put to it, he could still handle a hurley with style and skill. Yet, with all that, he had about him the *gravitas* of much learning and experience. People still talk about him in Dalkey and Killiney, fully a generation after his time.

So it was no surprise to me that he should be the doyen of the company in the Druid's Chair that night when the subject of the Lane pictures came up. These, the property of Irishman, Sir Hugh Lane, who went down with the *Lusitania* off the Old Head of Kinsale in 1917—a pretext for the United States entering the war—were held in London, though it was hotly contended that in a clear codicil to his will, they had been bequeathed by their owner to his native country, Ireland. The contention frequently erupted in the public arena, with regular political and diplomatic overtures being made to repatriate them. Some such move must have been afoot around that time.

Darcy, no stranger to the notion of 'perfidious Albion', would have been in no doubt as to whom the pictures properly belonged; in no doubt either that their sequestering by an acquisitive and heavy-handed British establishment was but yet one more example of the multitude of wrongs inflicted by their imperial majesties upon Mother Ireland. They were wrongs which he and a handful of others had gone out to right in 1916. So far as he was concerned, that fight was not over. The 'theft' of the Lane pictures was but one further aspect of it.

This, then, is the man from whom I first hear the name, Cyril Cusack. Suddenly—I relate Darcy's own account of it—a chair is flung backwards on the public house floor and Cyril is on his feet.

'Those pictures are ours', he declares. 'The bastards robbed them from us. And I'm going over there right now to get them back.'

There follows a moment of shocked silence while the others in the company seek to adjust to his truculent mood. They all know Cyril to be a fiery bit of goods, someone who would certainly be willing to try it. But who was going to try it with him? Denis O'Dea (husband of Siobhán McKenna) is there—an old IRA hand himself—as is Louis Dolan, a middle-aged solicitor with an ailing wife; both demur, saying—though not in so many words, Cyril being in the mood he is in—that it is a daft idea. But the fourth man, one Harry Webster, is also a person of urgent and incisive mind; he, like Cyril, is an actor and hence quick to respond to the theatrical mood. Both, having in their time been schooled by the strongly nationalist Christian Brothers—a schooling aided, let it be said, by frequent injections of the same national fervour from old campaigners like Paddy Darcy and Denis O'Dea—do not require much goading to fire them into action. Their indignation at the national affront of the 'stolen' pictures, bubbling away beneath the surface at all times, is at boiling point once Cyril gets steamed up. All of this is further compounded by the lavish measures of strong drink which the 'Druid', Mr Regan, is dispensing.

The plan is simple: they will go down to Dún Laoghaire there and then and catch the mailboat. That will get them to Paddington in London by eight the following morning. From there they go straight to the gallery where the pictures are held.

'We go in, we cut the canvasses from their frames with a sharp knife and bring them back here to show them to you tomorrow night before handing them over to the National Gallery.'

The older men, Darcy and O'Dea, men who had done deeds of daring in their time, express their concern that the plan is hasty and ill conceived; but Harry Webster, the same live wire and fiery particle that Cyril is, thinks it a brilliant idea. So, without more ado, they knock back their drinks and off they go.

What happens next is not recorded. The best account anyone has of it is that they do indeed get to the mailboat; they do indeed get to England; but of their progress from Paddington to the London art gallery there is no reliable record. What a night's sojourn in the bar of the creeking and ramshackle old *Princess Maud*, on top of what their earlier sojourn in the bar of the Druid's Chair had done, may be left to the imagination. Suffice it to say that, though they themselves in due course return, the Lane pictures do not come with them—fortunately, perhaps, bearing in mind what bleary eyes and unsteady hands with sharp knives might have done to priceless and unpurchaseable *objets d'art*. One might reasonably be grateful that this was one Irish rising that did not succeed.

It must have been about this time that the same Paddy Darcy, out for a stroll along the Vico Road one early Sunday morning, is confronted with a sight which he can scarcely believe. The Vico, with the woods and trees along the roadside, does indeed produce a plentiful supply of twigs and bits of broken wood which would be very good for fire-lighting. Strolling along the cliffside walk towards Dalkey, what he seems to see in front of him is a donkey and cart, with a man on foot out front leading the donkey and three young children in the cart behind him. In the Dublin of that time, the early Fifties, the sight of a donkey and cart is unusual; in the opulent suburb of Killiney, it might just as well have been the man on the moon.

The children, when he gets to them, turn out to be the

Cusacks—Paul, Sinéad and Sorcha; and the errand they are on, Cyril informs his friend, is to collect sticks to light the fire for their Mammy when they get home. All this is told with perfect earnestness; with some urgency too, since they must be back in time to have the fire lighting before she gets up. Living, as they are at the time in a fine bungalow on Sorrento Road—it is now millionaire country, but even then there was no shortage of money about—one may imagine what the affluent neighbours thought of a donkey and a cartful of children, out with their father to gather sticks for the fire. They might just as easily have been Snow White and the Seven Dwarfs out with their pickaxes digging for gold!

Killiney is where all this happens and it is where the Cusack girls cross my line of vision for the first time. As anyone who has ever seen the place knows, it is a singularly beautiful place: the magnificent range of the Wicklow Mountains draped across one end, with the Mugglins, Dalkey Island and the tip of Vico Point at the other. It has been compared to the Bay of Naples—hence, some of the local names, Sorrento, Vico, Mount Mapas. Shaw lived at Torca Cottage above the Vico, still there to the good for all to see. In *John Bull's Other Island* he has someone saying that 'the men of Ireland are temporal and mortal but her hills are eternal'. About the hills at least he is right: from the Torca vantage point where he saw them day by day as a young man, it is a majestic sweep rising out of the sea, silent and sublime, a still frame caught for all time and eternity. From the top of Killiney Hill on a clear day you can see Snowdon and the Welsh mountains; and, away to the north, Cúchulain country, Slieve Gullion, Slieve Donard and the Mountains of Mourne. The young Cusacks grew up in this place and it is there for the first time that I get to meet them.

This is on a June day in 1964, a short time after I have left the civil service and gone to work in RTÉ. By then the language has come to have an important place in our family life, largely through the influence of the all-Irish Scoil Lorcáin, where we send the children to school. To help them along, I speak Irish with them when we are out together; which is pretty well what I am doing this June day in 1964, as we go romping through Killiney Wood. The day is fine, the place is pleasant, the atmosphere is carefree and happy; and here we were, having fun with each other 'as Gaelige'. Suddenly, up the footpath leading into the wood comes this group of teenagers, boys and girls, probably just about finishing their Leaving Cert. As they come nearer, I see at a glance that two of the girls are stunningly beautiful, each with a mane of ash-blond hair and faces like Michelangelo angels. There are others, but this pair stands out. What comes to mind are the lines from an ancient fable about the Danaan Princess Éadaoin, stolen away to Tara to become bride to the High King, but ever after sought by her Danaan lover Mir who cannot live without her:

> *A ainnir fionn, an rachaidh tú liom*
> *Go tír na n-iontas, tír an cheoil,*
> *Is slaod den samhaircín folt gach aoinn' ann,*
> *Is sneachta aon-gheal gach corp gan gó.*

> *My fair-haired one, I beg you to come,*
> *Come back with me to Tír na nÓg,*
> *A primrose shower crowns every head there,*
> *Each body pure as driven snow.*

A bhean, má théann tú liom don tír sin,
Beidh mionn den ór-bhuí ar do cheann;
Lionn is leamhnacht, mil is fíon,
Má théann tú liom, a ainnir fionn.

But fly with me to our own homeland
And wreaths of gold shall be your crown;
Wine and milk, love, mead and honey,
If you'll but come, my fair-haired one.

These solemn verses come to life as this pair of 'vision-women' begin to speak to us.

'Dia's Muire dhaoibh! Tá Gaeilge agaibh?'

'Cinnte, tá Gaeilge againn,' I say. 'Bhfuil Gaeilge agaibhse?'

'Go deimhin tá, agus neart,' they tell me—and go on to prove it.

Now it so happens that at that time I know most of the Irish-speaking families in the area—if for no other reason than that there aren't all that many. But I do not know them.

'Cad is ainm daoibh?'

'Ní Chíosóig. Sinéad agus Sorcha Ní Chíosóig.'

I know no Cíosóigs' in the Scoil Lorcáin circle, the only place where Irish as natural as that would be likely to be found.

'Ní Chíosóig? Sin Cusack i mBéarla?'

'Sea cinnte. B'fhéidir go bhfuil aithne agat ar ár n-athair, Cyril. Is aisteoir é.'

Well, as the saying goes, that is the start of it. RTÉ at the time is looking for continuity announcers, bilingual ones preferably. So I invite them in for an audition and a screen test. They come—and are as near perfect as anyone could want them to be.

'Ask them how soon they can start,' Head of Presentation,

Pádhraic Ó Raghallaigh, tells me. 'What training they may need can be given to them between live sessions on air.' So it becomes my pleasant task to tell them the good news. But I have a surprise coming. For, prestigious and much sought after as the job of continuity announcer on television may be, it is not sought after by their wise and thoughtful mother.

'They've just started university,' she tells me. 'I don't want them distracted from that until they've finished what they set out to do.'

I try to persuade her, saying that we can arrange for it to be part-time, so they can continue with their university work unimpeded. But the lady is not for turning.

'Performance is a fickle old game,' she explains. 'As we in this house well know, you can never tell what may happen from one week to the next. We would just like to see them finish their education before they go down that road.'

I go back to Pádhraic Ó Raghallaigh to tell him the bad news. 'Talk about looking a gift horse in the mouth!' I say. 'They'd have been made for life.'

'They might,' he agrees. 'On the other hand, they might not. Maureen may be right. Even gift horses can kick. I know—having been kicked by a few!'

It was not to be the end of their association with RTÉ. Later, I cast them as often as I can in support roles—they could have had the main ones if they wished; this is in the Irish language series 'Labhair Gaeilge Linn', presented by the vibrant and volatile Eoin Ó Súilleabháin. The programmes are set in a modern apartment block. What with the stylish decor and the even more stylish girls, it begins to dawn on viewers, young people especially, that Irish need not mean the 'pig in the parlour' any more, but can be right up there with the most stylish and best. To Sinéad and Sorcha Cusack—later, their younger sister Niamh too—some small part of the credit for that turnabout must go.

So it is that I get to know the Cusack girls and their mother, Maureen, long before I get to know Cyril himself. (Now that I am on the theme, I had better say that, one day shortly after I have got to know him, I make some complimentary remark about a performance of hers in the Peacock Theatre, which he shrugs off in a surprisingly cold and unfriendly way: 'Things have not been what they used to be there,' he says. 'Maureen and I have had a bit of an estrangement.' And, for further clarity, I had better also say that I never get to know the fourth Cusack girl at all—Catherine, the child of a new relationship. In time, she will turn up on the boards herself, and with some success too. Though I do remember, years later, seeing her arm in arm with her father on the pier in Dún Laoghaire in what was clearly a happy father–daughter relationship.)

The reason I get to meet Cyril at last has nothing to do with him at all, but with his and Maureen's youngest daughter, Niamh. She, like the others, had been to the all-Irish Scoil Lorcáin, and thence to the secondary all-Irish Coláiste Íosagáin in Stillorgan. Some of my own children are in the same class with her there; and at a Christmas party one year, I hear her play the concert flute—it is the haunting air for the Communion hymn made popular by Seán Ó Riada and Cór Chúil Aodha in his 'Aifreann Gaeilge', Tadhg Gaelach Ó Súilleabháin's 'Gile mo Chroí do Chroí-se, a Shlánuitheoir'.

Everything the Cusacks did they did with perfection; here now is the third of them, a sylph like her sisters, with the same blond hair and her mother's starlit eyes, playing the silver flute with angelic grace, every note answering to the syllables of Tadhg Gaelach's rhapsodic celebration:

Gile mo chroí do chroí-se, a Shlánuitheoir,
Is ciste mo chroí do chroí-se d'fháil im chóir;
Ós follas gur líon mo chroí led ghrásta, a stór,
I gcochall mo chroí do chroí-se fág I gcomhad

Light of my life, sweet Saviour I adore,
My treasure in life is to love you more and more;
Since out of your heart great love for me
      you did pour,
Entwined in your heart be my heart for evermore.

Niamh is no more than 14 years old at that time, but it is quite plain to me that she is going to be a star. She does indeed go on to be a superb flautist; but, as the Spanish mystic St John of the Cross has it about *his* craft of poetry, she 'left the flock that she was tending'—to take to the stage, like her sisters and parents before her. And a highly accomplished performer she becomes too—as anyone who saw her in the part of Irena in Chekhov's *Three Sisters* will know; or, at the lower but more popular level, as the young doctor in the ITV soap, *Heartbeat*.

My bilingual 'Trom agus Éadrom' is running at the time and, in this exquisite rendition of 'Gile mo Chroí', I see a perfect item for it, a headline in what I am trying to make the programme: a celebration of all that is unique and lovely in the Irish language and native culture. So I ask her to come on to the very next show, which happens to be a Christmas one. Then it occurs to me that it would make an interesting turn to have her father along—to talk about what Christmas meant to him when he was her age.

This bit of the story bears telling—if for no other reason than that it shows a side of Cyril Cusack which came as a surprise to others who knew him when I told them. He was out of the country at the time, but his agent to whom I put the proposition came back to me to say that 'Mr Cusack will get in touch with you himself.' He does. He is in Italy on location but will be back in London for Christmas. When I tell him the date, he says yes, he can make that. Then I mention the word 'fee'. He says I am not to even think about it—though I am not to tell his agent he said so! He will be quite happy to do the show if we simply book him a return flight from London, ordinary fare, and pay him whatever we can after that.

'When it's for something to help the Irish language,' he tells me, 'just say when and where you want me and, if at all possible, I'll be there.'

This is in such marked contrast to the gossip I had heard before and since about what some referred to as his legendary meanness—much of it, I have to say, from his own theatrical fraternity—that I tell it here in order to show that it was no part of the man I came to know. For this would be the beginning of a warm and enriching friendship which will last right up to the time he dies.

That Christmas 'Trom agus Éadrom' goes splendidly. Niamh plays 'Gile mo Chroí' as exquisitely as I knew she would; Cyril speaks about his early memories, including some Christmas carols I have not heard before. But what I recall especially about the night is something that had nothing at all to do with the programme itself—though, predictably, like everything else about the show, it did have a Christmas touch. This is a poem which I had just read in *The Listener*, some verses from which I already had by heart, so easily was it remembered. So I come out with it at the drinks session afterwards. The poem, 'O Billy, Do You Hear That Bell?' is by a writer I have never heard of, one Charles Causley.

Cyril claps his hands with delight when he hears the name: it turns out that Charles Causley is a friend of his in London. I like to recall that story because it makes the point that the best tribute you can pay a poet is to say that, though you never learned his poem at school or anywhere else, you can say it word-perfect, just from memory because you love it. It is certainly true in this case. So, in celebration of Charles Causley, and in memory of Cyril Cusack, for what it's worth, here it is:

> *O Billy, do you hear that bell*
> *Speaking from the spire?*
> *Has Willie Fell gone down the well*
> *Or is it fire, fire?*
> *And do you see a cinder star*
> *Sizzling in the sky,*
> *And crazy kings with burning wings*
> *Learning how to fly?*
>
> *O sister, soft as any shawl*
> *The sharp snow winds the wire,*
> *Pale as a pall the cattle trawl*
> *Their breath about the byre.*
> *Now in the rare and eating air*
> *The bird chinks on the thorn,*
> *And slowly through the holy blue*
> *The shepherd hauls his horn.*
>
> *O father, is that cruel cry*
> *Coming from the mire*
> *A Wise Man lost in the world's frost*
> *Or is it only Squire?*

And when the alleluia boys
Drum their December din,
Why do you call the constable
That he may lock them in?

O mother, who will find the flock
And harness up the shire,
And who will lock the weather-clock
If winter does not tire?
O who will ship a farthing dip
Upon the drifting day,
And seize a spark from heaven's dark
To burn the night away?

O Billy, will you wag the word
From off your freezing tongue,
Nor hire the hearse or district nurse
Because I am so young?
And shall we push the business on
And do the best we can
To cut free from the Christmas tree
The hanging, holy man?

On that programme, on other programmes we do together afterwards, Cyril always tries to speak such Irish as he can, though he is clearly out of touch. But, like others of his generation who took their Irish from the Christian Brothers, there is a genuine love for the language there and a willingness to try his hand at it as often as he can. He will occasionally say during our chats together how much he envied his old Synge Street school pal, Cearbhall Ó Dálaigh, who had managed to keep in close touch with the language during a busy legal and judicial life. Fluent or not, one could be in no doubt about his own sense of affection. Once, when we are on that theme, I remember coming out with what he will afterwards refer to as my 'Doubting Thomas' idea: after the Apostle Thomas has refused to believe that the Lord had risen until he can see the wounds in his flesh, he chastises him with the reproof, 'Blessed are they, Thomas, who have not seen and have believed.' Such people are surely akin to the great mass of our own folk who, though they do not have much Irish themselves, nevertheless want their children to have it, instinctively seeing in it the true mark of an indelible Irish identity.

But, like many of that generation, he can write Irish far better than he can speak it; for instance, this is the letter he writes to me from London when 'Trom agus Éadrom' is suddenly and without my knowledge taken off air:

9 Lughnasa '85
A Liaim, a chara dhíl,

Is oth liom go mór-mhór a léigheamh 'sa páipéar annso indé go bhfuil druim láimhe tugtha do 'Trom agus Éadrom' ag RTÉ agus a rádh go raibh sin déanta taobh thiar de do dhruim féin—is náireach an scéal é. Ana-dheacair a thuiscint agus chomh tábhachtach dúinn go léir is a bhí an clár céadna, dúinn-ne ná fuil an teanga chomh h-éascaidh sin againn.

Níl fágtha le rádh againn ach go mbeidh lá eile ag an bPaorach agus agat féin.

Le gach beannacht agus deagh-mhéinn.
Cyril

Quite by accident, some time before that, we meet one night while he is walking up Merrion Square in the direction of his then home in Hatch Street. Doheny and Nesbitt's is near by, familiar haunt of the republic of writers and artists—and various other hangers-on of Shakespeare's 'harlotry of players'. We go in for a drink, the bar manager sensibly directing us to the snug, where he promptly shoots the bolt to ensure that 'Dr Cusack' will be spared the enthusiasm of well-intentioned fans. (Incidentally, he hated being called 'Doctor' which, he said the day he was conferred with cap and gown, made him look like 'a clown in a circus with a floppy hat and Joseph's multicoloured overcoat!')

What follows in there that night are some of the most pleasant hours of conversation I have ever had: quiet and reflective, with bits and pieces of poetry thrown in. Ever since he had come to sense, he tells me, his big ambition in life was to be a poet, not an actor, a trade of which he seems not to approve all that much. Later on, when he plays the role of the long-lost Uncle Peter in *Glenroe*, he cannot walk ten yards of the road anywhere in Ireland without people coming up to him to shake hands and tell him what a great fellow he is. He becomes a star overnight—after fifty years at the game! It is what Peadar O'Donnell, quoting from *As You Like It*, used to refer to as 'the bubble fame'.

When he does eventually produce a book of poems, it fails to make any real impact; it is repetitious, sentimental, full of vague but unsuccessful imagery. But that night in Doheny and Nesbitt's there is no doubting the poetic thrust. Each time he comes out with a piece from a favourite poem, it is followed by a silence in which he seems to be savouring it. I feel as near then as I ever will be to the idea of the 'anam-chara', the soul-mate, listening to the heartbeat of a friend.

This was the idealistic, star-gazing Cyril Cusack, the one

Maureen Keely had fallen in love with long ago. Had others ever seen that side of him at all? I have heard him called all sorts of things—bad tempered, irascible, selfish, acquisitive, mean, cynical; in one case which really shocked me, 'an ugly embittered man'. That was certainly not the Cyril Cusack I knew; rather the delicately poised, caring soul I was with that night, made sensitive by some mortal wounding in his past, a wounding which hurt most of all perhaps because, in the process, he himself had wounded others in the same way.

As we part, I see him walking up Baggot Street, a sad, downcast, lonely-looking soul; and the lines of one of those poems which he has said with such feeling earlier come back to me:

> *Sunset, and evening star,*
> *And one clear call for me!*
> *And may there be no moaning of the bar,*
> *When I put out to sea ...*
>
> *Twilight and evening bell,*
> *And after that the dark!*
> *And may there be no sadness of farewell,*
> *When I embark;*
>
> *For tho' from out our bourne of Time and Place*
> *The flood may bear me far,*
> *I hope to see my Pilot face to face*
> *When I have crossed the bar.*

But his 70th birthday is coming up and, before leaving him, I ask if he will agree to do a celebration programme on 'Trom agus Éadrom'. It turns out to be a great joyous night, with him at the centre of an illustrious company—including one André de Vogelaere, then Belgian Ambassador to Ireland. Ireland is in the EEC by now and at midnight this André does the honours by bringing in the New Year in all the languages of Europe, Irish included. To finish it off, Cyril comes in with this parting shot: "'Beidh lá geal gréine in Éirinn fós" a dúirt Iarla Thír Eoghain sa Róimh fadó. Solas na bhFlaitheas dá anam—tá an lá sin ag teacht!'

But time is pressing and we are all getting on. Whenever he comes to Dublin in those last years, he stays in his house on Mulgrave Terrace in Dún Laoghaire, a pretty enough little place but hopelessly cluttered with the bric-à-brac and heirlooms of the long years. Is it the gloom and darkness of that place that drives him out of it so often, down to the East Pier in Dún Laoghaire where I sometimes meet him, communing with himself, all alone. For someone who had always looked so young and sprightly—surely at his best he *was* 'the only playboy of the western world'—there is no doubting the onset of old age. Occasionally during those years he will come into the Forty Foot, not so much to swim, but to sit around basking in the evening sun.

These are the twilight years; I just hope they held some light for him. Though, even now as I write about them, I am troubled by the thought that they did not. Despite all the success, the fame and fortune, the 'plaudits of the multitudes', it seemed to me that there was a lonely little man in there, crying out for understanding and forgiveness—forgiveness for what God knows, for I do not.

Our talk in those quiet evenings as the sun goes down behind the Dublin hills is always in Irish which, in Cyril's case, if anything, seems to get better as he gets older. More than once I have the fancy that when he comes back to Dublin he takes out some of the Synge Street school books and, as only an actor could, goes through them, restocking his mind and his vocal chords with the old familiar sounds.

One of those afternoons, I suggest to him that we go on a visit to his old friend, Paddy Darcy, with whom I started this memoir. He is living all alone now in the old homestead in the quarry below Dalkey Hill. So, one day after lunch together in Killiney, we go down—to find him in a scene of utter desolation. Cyril has brought a bottle of sherry—Darcy is not a drinker—and as we talk together he asks me, with old-world courtesy, to get Cyril and myself a drink. There is nothing to drink from but a few old cracked cups which I rinse under the tap in the hundred-year-old kitchen sink. It is a sad, broken-down life; but the talk that follows is like something out of the *Odyssey*, with the aged Odysseus at home to two of his loyal followers. What will remain graven on my memory for ever is something Cyril says about an old schoolmaster who had touched him with a love of poetry long ago, so much so that there are lines he can still remember from that time:

Locksley Hall that in the distance overlooks the sandy tracts,
And the hollow ocean-ridges roaring into cataracts.
Many a night from yonder ivied casement, ere I went to rest,
Did I look on great Orion sloping slowly to the West.

He has no sooner come out with this than Paddy Darcy joins in. 'That's Tennyson,' he says. 'The poor fellow was mad about his cousin, but she couldn't marry him. The rigidity of religion in those days! There are verses following those which are even more beautiful. Would I be boring you if I were to say them?'

Cyril looks at me and I at him: here is this blind old man, probably soon to die, who is going to recite some lines from a poem he probably never learned at school, just simply read it so often out of love that it stayed with him, word-perfect to this day. And he is asking Cyril Cusack—certainly the most celebrated Irish theatrical name then around—if he will be bored by it! Boredom is about the last thing in his mind; from the look of him, I can see that tears would be nearer the mark:

Many a night I saw the Pleiads, rising thro' the mellow shade,
Rising like a swarm of fire-flies tangled in a silver braid.

When the centuries behind me like a fruitful land reposed;
When I clung to all the present for the promise that it closed:

When I dipt into the future far as human eye could see:
Saw the vision of the world, and the wonder that would be.

In the spring a fuller crimson comes upon the robin's breast;
In the spring the wanton lapwing gets himself another crest;

In the spring a livelier iris changes on the burnished dove;
In the spring a young man's fancy turns to thoughts of love.

Whether it is so or not, I like to remember that as the last time I will be with Cyril Cusack. Our friend, Paddy Darcy, dies shortly afterwards; his house under the Quarry has now gone, replaced by a ring of luxury villas in the long garden under the rock-face where, all through the summer and autumn in Darcy's time, a glorious array of dahlias bloomed. But as we know, flowers fade and Darcy's dahlias under

Dalkey Hill are no exception. Even then, as he sees us out in the gathering dusk, there they are in the garden beyond, a symbol of a life that had once been so full of colour, now aged, dying and falling into decay.

'There is a flower that bloometh when autumn leaves are dead', sings Wallace in *Maritana*. For me, one such flower is the memory of that late October night when two friends came together in a shambles of an old house. It is a memory that will last.

Dublin Made Me

DR C. S. (TODD) ANDREWS

odd Andrews was thought to be a strong man, well capable of making unpopular decisions. The first time I consciously become aware of this is when, as CIÉ chairman, he decides that rail stations and bus destinations should have their names displayed in Irish as well as English. By that time, for a generation or more, he has been a driving force in the economic life of Ireland. He was central to the development of three major industries: tourism, turf and transport. But in some respects it is this clear and unequivocal direction about the CIÉ placenames that gives him a mass *public* image—one that, with the closure of Dublin's Harcourt Street line, will remain in people's minds long after far more substantial things are forgotten. In directing that placenames be in Irish, he is following a line often used by his friend, professor of history in Maynooth, Tomás Ó Fiaich; he would regularly say that the language was essential to an understanding of the topography, folklore and history of the places in which we live: the Falls Road in the heartland of nationalist Belfast is 'Bóthar na bhFál', the road of the hedges; the Shankill Road in the loyalist heartland is 'Bóthar na Seanchille', the road of the old church; and Belfast itself is 'Béal Feirste', the mouth of the 'fearsaid', the sand-bar across the Lagan on the way out of Belfast Lough.

This makes instant good sense to those with Irish, but little to the majority who do not. So it takes much courage and conviction on the part of one man to introduce an idea which will confront them with it everywhere they go. Todd Andrews, old freedom fighter that he is, has that courage and conviction. Protestations of love and favour for the language have been ten a penny since the foundation of the state, but there is little 'beart de réir do bhriathair' to follow on. Small wonder that the plain people should become disillusioned with the pretence, in some cases the downright hypocrisy, and should no longer believe that anything real or practical will be done. Here, at last, is someone who puts his money where his mouth is, to make one clear and simple decision, the results of which we see around us to this day. To visitors in Ireland, it is discernible proof that we are a separate nation with a language which is uniquely our own.

Some time after that, I put together ideas for a public seminar to be held in a large hall, at which the current state of the language and its future will be discussed. The principal speakers there will be, not so much the 'language enthusiasts', but people who, like Todd Andrews, have left their mark on the economic, social and cultural life of Ireland. The idea is that the practical-minded thrust that made those success stories is equally necessary for the language if it is to progress. Among the people I have in mind are Dr Andrews, Dr T. K. Whitaker, Brendan O'Regan, Archbishop Simms, Mícheál Mac Liammóir and Siobhán McKenna. The idea itself comes to nothing—shortly afterwards I leave the civil service to come to RTÉ; but in due course I do manage to get all those people on air on the same theme, and for a much wider audience.

'The evil that men do lives after them, the good is oft interred with their bones': Todd Andrews would have good reason to endorse the Shakespeare sentiment. Side by side with the rail and bus names, in some quarters he is best remembered for the closure of the Harcourt Street line. It is a blunder, say the pundits of hindsight, with road traffic in Dublin gone mad since and the centre city in daily danger of gridlock. But what has to be kept in mind is that gridlock was about the last thing in people's minds in the late Fifties when that decision was taken and when what was on the country's mind was not gridlock but bankruptcy. It was then that Seán Lemass gave Todd Andrews the unenviable task of making the railways pay; that, or close them down. Over a period of no more than five years, he would bring about fundamental changes in employee and management attitudes; and, by personal sorties into the running of CIÉ, would manage to reduce a massively loss-making network by a third—and so save its life.

This then is the man who in time comes to succeed Éamonn Andrews as chairman of RTÉ. Naturally something of the same dynamic was expected. But the two situations were totally different—CIÉ a heavy loss-maker, RTÉ a highly profitable one. Director General Kevin McCourt, a man with a proven track record as a business manager, shocked a staff gathering one day by telling them that the main criterion of success in the organisation was profitability. When challenged by some of the more vocal of the public service broadcasting fraternity among us, he goes on to say that, if it is not profit-making, it will quickly become loss-making—and spiteful governments will step in to wipe out whatever independence the public service people may have.

The argument goes on for quite some time within the hallowed halls. Meanwhile, down in the ranks the more basic argument prevails—what kind of programmes and programme content do we want? If we are to be what the founding statute calls us—a national broadcasting service—then *national* broadcasting is primarily what we should be about. Instead, we seem to be regularly doling out a mid-Atlantic pot-pourri, miles from our own national culture and life. Éamonn Andrews, good broadcaster that he was, had come from a mixture of that mid-Atlantic idiom with lavish dollops of Anglo-Saxon attitudes thrown in; early programme management and production people, crucial to the make-up of a television schedule, were even more markedly so.

Now, at last, we have this chairman who had grown up with the Arthur Griffith ethic of 'Sinn Féin', the self-reliance of 'ourselves alone'. Furthermore, he is a man who has seen three other major national enterprises through to successful times. Under his leadership, we think, the same will happen to us; not perhaps so much in the financial sense, where things are going well, as in the more basic matter of programme orientation and content.

One small incident which happens shortly before Todd Andrews's name comes forward will suffice to point up the sense of inferiority which seemed to allow that mid-Atlantic/Anglo-Saxon idiom to prevail. This concerns the appointment of a supervising film editor, an important post with an aesthetic dimension by all means, but not a top-ranking one in the overall set-up. No one seems to fit the bill from within the ranks, so the post is advertised in the broadcasting press, especially the BBC and ITV. Some names are short-listed, all foreigners; in the event, none of them is willing to come and relinquish established posts. So it is to be advertised again, this time with a more attractive package.

At the programmes meeting at which this is announced, I

ask whether someone cannot be found—or trained—from within the ranks of RTÉ to do the job. Successful films had been made in Ireland by Irish people before—Colm Ó Laoghaire, George Morrison (*Mise Éire*), Louis Marcus and Paddy Carey had all made films of note; what editors had edited their work? Surely one of them could be found, if necessary further trained, to fill this supervisory post? We have an airline run by Irishmen; transport, tourism and fishing industries are run by Irishmen; surely we can find an Irish person to do this comparatively straightforward job?

Controller Gunnar Rugheimer calls off the meeting and summons me to his office. Do I realise the implications of what I am saying, he asks. That, in particular, if a supervising film editor has to be Irish, then so too should a programme controller. Frankly, I say, yes, that indeed is the ideal (prophetically, as it turns out, it will happen shortly afterwards). What neither of us knows is that names are going into the hat for a new RTÉ Authority right then, the five year term of the first one having expired; and in selecting them the very thing I have been talking about will come very much into focus—a national orientation of which the Irish language and culture will form a central part. Among the members of the new authority, when it is announced, are Dr Andrews as chairman, Gael Linn's Dónall Ó Móráin, Phyllis Bean Uí Cheallaigh (widow of former President Seán T. Ó Ceallaigh), Ruairí Brugha (son of Cathal Brugha) and trade unionist Seán Ó Murchú.

So a new emphasis towards distinctively Irish programming is now confidently expected. And indeed some such programmes do happen: 'The Course of Irish History', 'Buntús Cainte', 'Watch Your Language' and 'Voices from a Hidden People'. But overall it is nothing like what some of us had expected. In some respects, that may have been just as well. For what good would it have done if an Irish language element were to become a regular feature of 'The Late Late Show', when the viewership that followed the show did not want it? Indeed, that would have smacked of the kind of forced feeding in the schools which had turned many against the language over the years. Yet, not long after Todd Andrews had taken up office, his secretary, Oliver Maloney, announces to an Irish language meeting in Dún Laoghaire that a new, more positive approach to the language will be adopted from then on: that, for one thing, a bilingual element will become a feature of entertainment shows. Will that include 'The Late Late?', someone asks. Indeed it will, he replies, very assuredly too. Well, the questioner says, we have heard that kind of talk before and nothing came of it. How can we be sure that it will happen now?

'Because my chairman said so,' Oliver stoutly asserts. 'In words of one syllable too. Anyone who knows my chairman knows what those words were.'

Well, as we know, it did not happen, either then or later; which, as I say, may have been just as well. But it was the kind of peremptory first-strike that the decisive Todd Andrews was capable of. It would give a clue to the meaning of a cryptic remark by Assistant Director General John Irvine, the most astute and observant of the senior executives in RTÉ at that time: 'Todd's second thoughts are often very far from his first!'

It was perhaps as well that they were. Whatever hopes and ambitions he may have had for creating new directions in broadcasting, based on his own tried and trusted philosophy of a resourceful, self-confident Ireland, they stood a small enough chance against the tidal wave of mid-Atlantic/ Anglo-Saxon culture that was everywhere about us. The trouble was that it was not all coming from outside. The fact is that when Douglas Hyde and Eoin MacNeill set up the Gaelic League three-quarters of a century before, with the 'de-Anglicisation of Ireland' as its aim, they were attempting to reverse a trend which had gone on for several centuries, with all the power and influence of government behind it— ever since the fourteenth century, in fact, when the Statutes of Kilkenny set out to wipe out every visible and audible sign of a distinctive Irish nation. In later times that would be aided by the so called 'national' schools which, well before the turn of the twentieth century, attempted to brainwash Irish children into believing that their best ambition would be to make them perfect replicas of their 'happy' counterparts across the water:

> *I thank the goodness and the grace*
> *That on my birth have smiled*
> *To make me in these pleasant days*
> *A happy English child*

RTÉ was, of course, no different from the rest of the country in all this, its staff being much the same as one would find in any other public company; but where the difference came— and comes—is in the crucial effect personality has on programme orientation and content. In my case, I had come from the civil service where this made little difference to one's work; any of a number of people doing a particular job would have done it pretty well the same and with the same results. But in television, the content and orientation of one's personal ideas and attitudes can and does make a whole world of difference between one person's handling of an idea and another. In a word, the message delivered depends a great deal on the attitude and personality of the one delivering it. Or, as Marshall McLuhan so succinctly put it all those years ago: 'the medium is the message'—the medium being the person through whom the message is delivered.

So when one got to be sitting on top of the pile, as Dr Andrews then was, and one wanted 'the message' i.e. the programmes to bear some resemblance to the message he wanted given, then he had better deliver it himself, or get people like him to do it for him. His problem was that few enough people in the RTÉ of his time were like him or had the same ideas as he had; fewer still shared to any appreciable extent his classically republican vision of a distinctive Irish culture with an educated self-confidence in its native worth.

All this was true especially in the area of 'contrived' programming, which certainly includes the whole range of cultural and entertainment output; to some extent, even to programmes of current affairs and contemporary comment too. When a producer is assigned to a programme in those areas, what appears on air will certainly reflect the kind of person he or she is. So, for example, a series of personality face-to-face interviews will turn up a wholly different set of interviewees from one producer to the next, even to the point where the subjects one will choose will be the direct opposite to the other's choice. What this boils down to is that the crucial area in which programme content and orientation is fixed is not at all at the later stage of programme and schedule planning, but at the much earlier stage of staff recruitment. One gets programmes in accordance with the personality and proclivities of the producers and back-up staff one selects. I rather doubt that Todd Andrews ever really understood this. Having come from the more straightforward world of industry and commerce, where the matrix-stamp of individual personality does not so centrally define the nature of the product, it is hard to blame him.

I become aware of this early on when he interviews me for the job of secretary to the authority. It is not a job I much want, but it is one where I feel I can influence the content of the programme schedule more effectively. Todd is not very long in office at this time; I have been there some years. In that time I have come to the view that only very clear and unequivocal guidelines from an authority can do anything effective to help implement what the governing statute refers to as the 'national culture', including the language. This, I feel, is where an experienced programme-maker can make a meaningful contribution to authority policy and thinking. The illustrious chairman does not feel that way at all.

When pressed to say why I want the job, I reply that, since what RTÉ is supposed to be about is programmes, I want to contribute thoughts on the programme strands and concepts which national broadcasting should be about. This can very credibly be done while keeping the balance between the governing imperatives of 'education, information and entertainment'. I would also, I go on, want to put forward ideas on how the authority can give clear cultural leadership in those fields so as to point the programme-planners in the directions they favour. They are, after all, the custodians of the public interest, to reflect in their programmes what the statute has put them there to do. By all means they should do this with discretion and sensitivity so as not to limit individual freedom and creativity on the production side.

All the time I am sounding off like this, I am conscious of his eyes on me: two sapphire-blue eyes with centre-points of sparkling flint. I can see myself being critically assessed by an unusual man, someone who in his time has seen the terrors of the Black and Tan War, who served with Michael Collins's hit-men of the Dublin Brigade on Bloody Sunday morning, someone too who, later, piloted three major national industries through stormy times into the calm waters of peace and prosperity. He is, we have been told, a man who does not suffer fools gladly. Yet here now is this 'fool' rushing in 'where angels fear to tread', though perhaps not so much a fool as a kind of latter-day 'Dalek' from 'Dr Who', making sounds and noises which are utterly foreign to the man listening to him. In a word, by the time I finish I know I have not got the job. If I retain some tiny measure of hope, I am quickly disabused of it when he tells me—in those words of one syllable of his!—that what he wants from a secretary to the authority is not some high-sounding broadcasting philosopher but 'someone who will sit quietly at meetings and take the notes'. It would be less than fair to me if I were to pretend that, when I applied for the job, that was any small part of what I wanted; that, in effect, would have landed me back with the impotent 'castrato' role of my earlier civil service life!

But perhaps, more importantly, I then also came to the view that however effective a chairman Todd Andrews had been in guiding other national enterprises to success, he would have little or no influence on the kind of changes in programme content and orientation I had in mind; and, further still, to the view that while the commercial and business side of a television service is indeed crucial to its continuing life, the overall management of its affairs is best achieved by people who have spent at least some time at the coal-face working at the trade and, because of that, whose creative corpuscles are fully alive to its personal vagaries.

Having said that, I also have to say that in selecting the secretary he did appoint, Oliver Maloney, he made a very good choice. Oliver, like me, had also been a civil servant; had in fact for a time been private secretary to the chairman of the Revenue Commissioners where—again like me in the years I spent with Seán MacEntee—he must have seen some pretty lively fireworks. He had a cool head and even cooler speech, both attributes that stood him in good stead in the sometimes stormy sessions that took place within and outside the boardroom. Occasionally too he had the unenviable task of keeping the lines of communication open between two very different personalities: the debonair, affable, courteous Kevin McCourt, and the straight-talking, gravelly, monosyllabic Todd Andrews. Only a very patient and astute man could have done that, and survive. And not only survive, but go on in due course to make a good director general himself, a role in which he lasted all too short a time. In that time he did seriously attempt to bring about some important changes—until the glutinous atmosphere in which RTÉ then was, caught up with him and he left.

• I may be pardoned for thinking that as time went on and that very atmosphere got to him, Chairman Andrews came to the view that there really was not much he could do to alter the course of things. To a close friend, one of the few trusted collaborators he had there, he confided one day in that charmingly frank way of his: 'There's fuck all I can do with that place!' From this groundling's view of things at the time, it was a sentiment with which I had some sympathy. Having put forward many realistic, carefully constructed papers proposing new and revised programme outlines, mainly regarding the language and national culture, and seen them die the death for lack of interest, I dolefully began to come around to the view that, in part at least, he might have been right, though maybe the real truth is that we all expect too much and, in our pilgrims' progress, are bound to be disappointed.

Nevertheless, some good things happened which might not have happened—or have happened with such express—

had he not been there. It is unlikely, for instance, that my language teaching series, 'Buntús Cainte', would have got the financial and facilities support it did but for the fact that TV Controller Gunnar Rugheimer was keen to have the chairman's approval for the renewal of his contract, which was imminent at the time. When, later, Todd himself, perhaps seeing in Gunnar something of a blood-brother, averred that he 'could have worked with that Swedish bear', he may have been thinking of the very positive and effective help he gave with projects like 'Buntús'. He was also chairman during the formative stages of 'Watch Your Language', a series aimed at re-educating the public in the importance of the language to the nation's life; and of 'Voices from a Hidden People', a splendid series aimed at showing how eighteenth-century poetry in Irish had mirrored the people's lives.

Those, though good efforts, were but a small part of the overall television output; and in any case they lasted only a few months at a time. So far as I was concerned, they were nothing like as satisfying as what I managed to do when I eventually got away from the idea of trying to affect the programme schedule as a whole and went on air myself.

This was with a little two/three-hander interview series called 'Gairm' shot in a few hours on Saturday morning in a corner of the 'Late Late' set. All goes fine for a season or so and then, one morning when I have as my guests Éamon de Buitléar ('Amuigh Faoin Spéir') and Gearóid Ó Tuathaigh (now Professor of History at UCG); my boredom threshold, never too high, is quickly reached. From his Ceoltóirí Chualann days and before that, Éamon, I know, always carries the tin whistle around with him; and Gearóid, I know, is a fine step-dancer—I had seen him on the boards of

Taibhdhearc na Gaillimhe with Celine Hession, one of the 'greats' of Irish dancing long before 'Riverdance' was heard of. There and then, I ask them to do a turn for me—a brazen piece of impromptu programming which, fortunately, works like a dream. Why not consider expanding the idea, I am asked by some of my lords and masters the following day, by getting an audience in and doing a weekly bilingual chat and entertainment show? Such are the slight beginnings of 'Trom agus Éadrom'.

After 'Trom' come the Eve of All Ireland shows, 'A Rich and Rare Land', 'Lifelines' and several others, none of them in my mind when I started out in television in the first place. That Marshall McLuhan lesson that 'the medium is the message' was certainly to prove true in my case. It is a lesson with which I feel Chairman Andrews, talented and versatile man though he was, never really got to grips. Yet here was I, after largely agreeing with him for years that 'you could do fuck all with that place', now doing things I really wanted to do—and doing them myself, a form of 'Sinn Féinery' that is surely familiar to all those who work in that strange, highly personalised territory, the republic of the media.

I don't think that either he or I ever got over the kind of instant antipathy that seemed to come down like a fire-curtain between us at that first meeting when he interviewed me for the job of secretary to the authority. There was something quite palpable in the air then which told me that we would never have got on—possibly a manifestation of that physics principle that 'likes repel, opposites attract'. This is not to say that he would not have heartily approved of the kind of programme ideas I had, especially on the language and cultural side. The fact is that he helped whenever he could. For instance, one day when 'Buntús Cainte' was at the planning stage, he sent Oliver Maloney down to me to ask if I could use much-needed additional finance to help set up and sustain a stylish publicity campaign—which I could and did. Another time, when the programme was on air, I got a phone call at home one night from Áras an Uachtaráin, with President de Valera, prompted by him, commenting on the programme and offering suggestions for its improvement. For me, it was an encouraging intervention—especially coming from someone who had started to learn Irish himself from O'Growney's *First Steps in Irish* in the 'Craobh an Chéitinnigh' classes of the Gaelic League long years before.

That said, the initial antipathy continued to be there. Once, at a lunch following an authority meeting, he was being regaled by that rugged, freedom-loving old Englishwoman, Chloe Gibson, who was head of drama at the time. The thrust of her discourse was that social unrest is a necessary preliminary to all political change. It was an idea much in vogue at the time, one of its proponents being a Father Kelly, a well-known Jesuit. Todd Andrews must have seen a good deal of social unrest in his time—in the Black and Tan years he had done his bit to create some of it himself! But, from his years in CIÉ and other national bodies, he would have had little patience with the rabble-rousing side of it, which was getting on for epidemic proportions in RTÉ right then. As ill-luck would have it, I happened to pass just as Chloe was getting into full flight and clearly in need of encouragement and support to get her there. So she calls on me to lend weight to her argument.

'There's Liam Ó Murchú, Chairman,' she says, 'a strongly national-minded Irishman. He knows I'm right.'

The proposition latent in this accolade is, of course, that Todd Andrews is not a strongly national-minded Irishman and so has to have that concept explained to him by a parvenu like me! It is the match to the powder-keg.

'Are you talking about Father Kelly of the Society of Jesus?' he asks.

Yes, Chloe says, it is that Father Kelly who had been making those points.

'Well, Miss Gibson,' he drives on, 'I have nothing to say about that crowd only that they, in their time, ruined more Irish boys than the English conquest did in seven hundred years. And what saved us from final extinction was the Christian Brothers and the Dublin working class.'

I have no idea what poor Chloe did to deserve this Exocet but if, as I suspect, it was aimed at least partly at me, then it certainly was aimed at the wrong man! I had never missed a chance, on television or elsewhere, of saying what a debt of gratitude several generations of us owed to the Christian Brothers; as for the working class, anyone who knew the least thing about me knew that, from my early years, I knew far more about it and at first hand than the comfortable middle-class Todd Andrews would ever know. The 'Dublin' bit did strike me as a bit strange—until I read the first part of his fine autobiography, *Dublin Made Me*. In this, he tells the story of his own early days, when they had a dairy business in the Gardiner Street area, centre of Dublin slumland, where the poverty and hardship so eloquently portrayed in the works of Seán O'Casey would have been all around them. Another icon in his political past would have been James Connolly, the labour leader, head of the Citizen Army and signatory of the Proclamation of 1916. All that might have given some clue to that colourful riposte of his to Chloe Gibson; but the main trajectory, I felt, was aimed at me—for daring to intrude myself into a discourse which was not going his way.

It was not to be all one-way traffic. Some time afterwards, I found myself a guest in the house of Aodhagán Ó Rathaile, a good friend of Todd's and a close collaborator in the formative days of Bord na Móna. Aodhagán would often tell me how much he approved what I was trying to do to popularise Irish with 'Trom agus Éadrom' and, with his cousin, Síle Humphreys, would regularly run language soirées at home in the 'Trom' idiom, in which people like himself could, without embarrassment, practise such Irish as they had in the company of fluent speakers. This night, he had a few of the 'great and famous' in, including Todd Andrews and former Tánaiste and Minister for Foreign Affairs, Frank Aiken. At some stage during the night, Todd—in a mood of some misanthropy (again, was this characteristic, or was I doing it?)—was deploring the lack of cultural concern in the country at large and in the administration in particular. Everyone and everything, he said, seemed to be geared to one thing and one thing only—to get in on the new wave of prosperity—the 'Celtic Tiger' of those days! This, he vehemently went on, was personified in some of the up and coming politicians, the 'mohair suit brigade'—Charles Haughey, Donogh O'Malley, Brian Lenihan—all ardent promulgators of Ken Whitaker's 'First Programme of Economic Expansion', the aim of which was to effect an annual increase of 4 per cent in the Gross National Product.

'What's wrong with the country right now,' he summarily concluded, 'is this bloody 4 per cent mentality.'

As on the day of that first interview I had with him, I could see his sapphire-blue eyes on me. Was I not of the same mind as them, substituting the glitz and glamour of television for things of substance and cultural worth? Well, perhaps I was. But I also had another view and one that was very definitely not in line with his.

'So far as I am concerned,' I say, 'there is only one thing wrong with the 4 per cent mentality, and that is that it should be an 8 per cent mentality. What's really wrong is that we have fallen down in our sense of nationhood, have turned our backs on the language and the native culture which were the mainspring of the fight for freedom. So small wonder that something like the 4 per cent mentality has come along to fill the vacuum.'

'A touch, a touch, I do confess'—Hamlet's remark at the rapier cut from Laertes might summarise Todd's response. There was much nodding of heads and some murmurs of assent. All of which might have left yours truly moderately chuffed but for the fact that his loyal spouse, after we have left them and are driving away, brings him down to earth with the chastening remark, 'You, love, are the darling of the has-beens!'

Dr Tom Murphy, later President of UCD, came to work in the Department of Health in the Custom House in the early Fifties. Before that he had been medical officer with Bord na Móna, where he had close contacts with its chairman, Todd Andrews. By family tradition he was Fine Gael and a close friend of Tom O'Higgins—later a Fine Gael Minister for Health and, later again, Chief Justice, while Todd Andrews was died in the wool Fianna Fáil, an ardent admirer of de Valera and Seán Lemass. But not the slightest hint of antipathy ever seemed to exist between them. Tom was never done speaking with admiration of Todd: a man of outstanding vision, he would say, who—unlike others of his time—had an intensely practical turn of mind. Once when there was a problem with pneumoconiosis, a potentially fatal lung disease to which coalminers and others working in a permanently dusty atmosphere are prone, urgent measures were needed to deal with it. For some of the workforce, it was already too late, nothing much could be done; but for the majority a great deal could. With immediate effect, Todd

Andrews proposed and had implemented a scheme of insurance, funded largely by the company, to guarantee workers' incomes while they were under treatment, a form of insurance well ahead of its time and the forerunner of later social and voluntary health insurance schemes. It was typical of the man, Tom Murphy would say, that it happened with the thoroughness and express that it did.

'Put half a dozen men like that in charge of the nation's affairs, instead of the rabble-rousers and pipe-dreamers we have, and there's a chance that we might become a nation once again.'

This was the dynamic which was repeated in the bigger and more complex fields of tourism and transport. That he did not have the same effect in RTÉ was, as I have said, no fault of his. He may have overstated things a bit when he confided to that friend of his that he 'could do fuck all with that place'; he could—but it would have taken a much longer time than he had to give it. In that time he would in all probability have managed to put people in place who had the vision, background and cast of mind to do the things he wanted done. By the time he became chairman, structures and people were already there; it is what *they* wished to deliver that would be delivered—which, alas, was often far from what he would have wished. His frustration, by the time he made that damning remark, might be compared to that of a good driver left sitting in the passenger seat, while being driven by a bad one in directions in which he did not want to go.

Anyway, his time in RTÉ ends abruptly when his son David is appointed a minister by Jack Lynch; in this role he might conceivably come into conflict with the RTÉ Authority which, his father being chairman, would not have made a pretty sight. In any case Todd is over 70 now and has small relish for the back-stabbing that broadcasting life can sometimes be—a phenomenon, incidentally, by no means confined to Ireland. The story goes that when a programmes executive with the BBC in Scotland arrived down in the London headquarters one day, he met up with a colleague who had once worked with him up north.

'Have they stopped stabbing each other in the back up there yet?' he is asked.

'My dear chap, they stopped that years ago. They're stabbing each other in the face now.'

So ended a long life of public service and Dr C. S. 'Todd' Andrews finally went into retirement. It was a retirement full of satisfying work. His two autobiographical books, *Dublin Made Me* and *A Man Of No Property* are mandatory reading for anyone who wants to know about the making and shaping of modern Ireland. Add to them the regular feature articles in the *Irish Press* under the editorship of Tim Pat Coogan—fine combative pieces which bore the stamp of the man he was: clear headed, single minded, a shade iconoclastic by all means and occasionally intolerant, but always with the core of practical patriotism which marked the whole of his life's work.

His friend Cardinal Ó Fiaich, in the homily at his funeral Mass, spoke of the dream of the Young Ireland visionary, James Fintan Lalor's Ireland 'free from the sod to the sky'. If there are protecting cohorts above us both now and in the time to come, Todd Andrews and Tomás Ó Fiaich will surely be among them. They and their likes have certainly helped bring us a shade closer to the realisation of that prophecy of the Great O'Neill, Earl of Tyrone, as he lay dying in Rome close on four centuries ago: 'Beidh lá geal gréine in Éirinn fós.'

'Múscail do Mhisneach'

CHARLES HAUGHEY

As I report in an earlier chapter in this book—the one on Seán MacEntee—twice in the course of my civil service life my path crosses with that of Charles Haughey. On both occasions this innocent abroad takes a tumble.

The third time, I have left the civil service and am in RTÉ, with the grandiose title of 'Editor of Irish Language, Social, Religious and Educational Programmes', a title with power in inverse proportion to its length. But, long as it is, it still has no hint of politics or current affairs. Yet for some reason which, at this distance, I cannot recall, I find myself landed with the job of handling party political broadcasts coming up to a general election. It is in this role that I present myself to the Fianna Fáil Director of Elections, then Minister for Finance, Charles J. Haughey. My brief is to outline to him the facilities RTÉ makes available for such broadcasts.

He is not alone. The formidable array of election folk around him includes two good friends—Eoin Ó Cionna, a consulting engineer with a big practice in Dublin, and Noel Mulcahy, Deputy Director General of the Irish Management Institute and Cathaoirleach of Comhairle na Gaeilge. 'Speak when you are spoken to' is a lesson I learned long ago as the youngest of a large family; so I sit there this day, silent and respectful, awaiting my turn to be called.

When eventually the turn comes, I say my piece briefly and without comment: studio dates and times, durations, autocue-scripts, press and *RTÉ Guide* billings—it is the same for all political parties. In total it takes perhaps five minutes.

'You don't sound too enthusiastic about it', a throaty growl comes at me from the head of the table. Well now, I think, it is not my business to sound enthusiastic about anything. What I am here to do is the simple job of relaying the facts, leaving it to him and his to make what they can of them.

'I mean you don't sound too enthusiastic about party political broadcasts. Am I right?'

My time in civil servitude has taught me to answer such questions with care, especially ones coming from the minister who is chiefly responsible for civil servants. Answer them by all means, truthfully and directly too, but not in a way that will lead to further questions, further traps, further trouble. Still, an answer I must give.

'Since you ask,' I say, 'they would not be my first choice for a night's viewing.'

True it indeed is but, to be honest, it is a great deal less than the truth. Party politicals preach to the converted, if even to them; for the rest—the great majority—they are a surefire switch-off.

'What would make you *not* switch them off?' I am pressed.

Contrary to that old civil service habit of keeping my trap shut, I fall for it. Like a moth to the light, I hear myself going on—about the drudge and the boredom of them, the predictable switch-off, even to the point of asking whether sensible political folk cannot think of better ways to spend their time and money. The illustrious director of elections, with his assembled faithful, sits there in what looks like a stunned silence: here is someone who is a practitioner in the trade telling them how little he thinks of the jewel in their crown. Warming to the theme, I ask if it might not be possible to inject a little life into them, something to stop viewers yawning at the first word and reaching for the switch button. If, for instance, the subject were agriculture, what would be wrong with an opening verse from the Land League ballad, 'The Bould Tenant Farmer'—to show how far the agricultural scene had advanced since the 'bould tenant farmer' days? Or, if the subject were Europe, what would be wrong with a brief résumé of Ireland's presence in Europe long centuries before a Common Market or a European Union was heard of? Anything but the repetition of dull facts which, even when given by the most personable talking head, is still the most boring way to present anything on television.

The meeting breaks up shortly afterwards and I am about to depart when my friends, Eoin Ó Cionna and Noel Mulcahy, who are still with the minister, call on me to join them. It is relevant to note that all three of us have a very considerable interest in the development of the language at the time—for which Charles Haughey, as Minister for Finance, has overall governmental responsibility.

'Where did ye dig up this fella?' he asks my friends. In reply, they say a word about my civil service background and, latterly, my work in television. Then, Noel Mulcahy adds a rider.

'That's what you've got to realise about the language now, Charlie. This is the kind of realistic get you'll be dealing with from now on—not decent well-meaning philanthropists like 'An Seabhac' and Aindrias Ó Muineacháin. But don't be misled by his nice, innocent-looking little face.'

'I won't,' Charles J. assures him. 'I might even have something to learn from his looking innocent!'

Our 'innocent-looking faces' next cross each other's line of vision some time later when I am attempting to launch a new language-teaching series on RTÉ, the one that will become 'Buntús Cainte'. This, the brain-child of linguistics expert Father Colmán Ó Huallacháin, would be a far more structured and ambitious venture than 'Labhair Gaeilge Linn' which had preceded it. As well as a television series, there would be radio programmes, records and cassettes and, hallmark of all well-made language-teaching programmes, a learner's booklet, complete with text, dictionary and a guide to phonetics and sounds—in a word, a prestige job, and one requiring a sound financial back-up—which is where the Minister for Finance comes in.

The Department of Education, under whose auspices the original 'Buntús' research work was done, persists for a time in believing that they are running the television programme— an impression, to be fair to them, which stemmed from the shock announcement in the *Sunday Independent* by their innovative free-fall minister, Donogh O'Malley, that a revolutionary new teaching series would shortly start up on RTÉ. No one was consulted, no one in RTÉ knew; just— bang!—suddenly, the programme will be there! A sheaf of papers lands on my desk with instructions to examine how a television series can be made of them. One look at this dry as dust and deadly repetitious set of lessons is enough to tell me that, short of a miracle, nothing can be made of them. Like those 'party politicals', here is another of those politically motivated rituals guaranteed to bore the viewers. Each lesson of the 180 before me would, I could clearly see, require a large lump of melted sealing wax stuck to the viewer's backside to compel him or her to sit down and endure looking at it for the time it would take—unless some miracle, some flight of luck or fancy, could save it.

Something did; this came in the form of a five pronged assault which would shatter it in pieces and make it work for television. In short order, the prongs were these: brevity, each programme five minutes long; peak viewing time, 7.55 p.m.; a catchy introduction both in music and pictures; clever illustrations, giving a laugh a line; and last but by no means least the providential arrival of the mini-skirt on the contemporary fashion scene. These latter would be displayed with such panache by the three lovelies presenting the programme that the holy saints of heaven could be forgiven for wanting to waste the necessary five minutes a night brushing up on their celestial Gaeilge.

With those ingredients, the dry as dust sheaf of lessons became alchemised into a TAM-topping television winner. But this in itself created problems, and problems RTÉ could not solve. The five minute slot at peak viewing time would hold an audience of close enough to a million viewers (there were no alternative channels then); families would certainly stay with it; so a booklet at a giveaway price was needed. At a shilling apiece (5 pence now) it would surely sell to at least a quarter of them. But who would pay for it? Programme-making was the business of RTÉ, not books or book-selling. As to the selling, Colmán Ó Huallacháin and I were at one that we should forget the classy bookshops, just try to get it into the big supermarkets and stores. At a shilling a shot, once you were in there, a print-run of a quarter of a million would pay the costs.

But where were those costs to come from? The Department of Education, neanderthal at the best of times, did not look kindly on the proposition that they should pay. Their people on the steering group damn nearly fell under the table when the quarter-million figure was mentioned. Such figures were in the inter-stellar regions; nobody counted that far! Something smaller might be possible. What might 'something smaller' mean? At the wild outside, we are told, maybe forty to fifty thousand; even that would be stretching things to the limit. I could see at once that the highly attractive promo-clips we had made to help sell both programme and booklet would serve only to create a public demand which could not be met. Better do nothing at all rather than build up frustration like that. Having an unwanted Irish language-teaching programme at peak time was bad enough without making people angry and frustrated about it as well.

This is where Charles Haughey comes in. Colmán, being the linguist he was, insisted that the booklet was necessary; being the innovator he was, he also insisted that we find a way around it.

'Aren't you friendly with Haughey?' he asks, as we stand at the gates of the Department of Education offices on Marlborough Street.

'I believe I could talk to him about it, if it will help.'

'It will. I'm going back right now to see what Minister O'Malley has to say. It was he who started this thing in the first place. Now he's going to finish it!'

He leaves me with this sanguine thought and I drive back to RTÉ. When I arrive fifteen minutes later, there is a phone call awaiting me. It is the old familiar growl.

'What's all this wild talk I'm hearing from O'Malley about some book of yours that's going to sell a million copies?'

I tell him the facts: that the programme will be short enough to hold an audience; that it will go out at peak viewing time; and that its viewership will indeed be close enough to a million. Allowing one book per four viewers, a quarter of a million is a fair guess. At a shilling each, the print-run will cover the cost. But somebody has to guarantee the cost. Will he? It takes as long to say this then as it has taken you to read it now. The response is instant.

'Go ahead. You have your book. I'll ring O'Malley and tell him I'll fix the money. But you'd better be right about those figures. Otherwise, your head is on the block!'

My head, I am glad to say, was not on the block. Before the first programme went on air, 238,000 copies of the 'Buntús Cainte' booklet were sold!

The next time my path crosses with that of Charles Haughey concerns a scholarly Jewish gentleman and a dance in a beautiful house. It comes about in this way.

Dr Meir Gertner, Professor of Talmudic Studies in the University of London, is also an expert on the teaching of Hebrew to adult Jews who want to go to Israel either on holiday or to live there. In an interview he did at the BBC during my time there, I heard him tell about the extraordinary achievement of making an all but dead language into a language of full modern technology within the space of two generations. It was surely an achievement which had lessons for us in Ireland.

So when I get to planning a television series about our language situation here, I think it might be a good idea to have him over as one of its presenters. The purpose of this series would be to demonstrate the central role of language in the preservation and development of a nation's culture. Even when that point was made, and successfully made, a more pressing question remained: how do you convince people, who have quite enough to do to make ends meet and get on with their lives, that they should take on the additional burden of language-learning—for the great majority, a language that had long since gone out of use in ordinary, everyday speech; the more especially since they now had English, a worldwide language, as the language of hearth and home?

The series of programmes in due course becomes 'Watch Your Language'; and Dr Meir Gertner presents the final one, 'A View from Outside'.

For this, he seeks out current attitudes to the language through newspaper and media editors, leaders in the secular and clerical world, and ministers charged with specific responsibility for implementing aspects of government policy, especially education and finance. That means an interview with the then Finance Minister, Charles Haughey.

Our initial exploratory meeting with him is marked by what everyone later comes to know as his 'grand seigneurial' style. When will Dr Gertner be free to come back to Dublin to conduct the interview? The date and time are fixed; then, with a wave of his hand, all further details are brushed aside: an ambassadorial car will arrive at his home in London to drive him to Heathrow for the flight to Dublin; there, a ministerial car will await him to drive him to Kinsealy, where cameras will be set up in an ante-room all ready for the interview, with lunch to follow in the baronial manor. It will be the same star-studded progress for the return journey. Meir Gertner—thrifty, modest, Jewish—is clearly impressed; I—plebeian, Christian (Brothers), Irish—am overwhelmed. If ever I saw it, this was 'Grand Seigneur Rule OK!'

The interview itself goes well. We have agreed in advance the areas for discussion, but no sooner has it started than Charles J. launches into a charming and delightful conversation piece—into which, however, he manages to inject some highly convincing personal points about the language and its signal importance as the mark of Irish nationhood. It is a brilliant, impromptu apologia; so much so

that when it comes on air a short time afterwards, some of
the more ardent of the language aficionados declare
themselves convinced by his sincerity. It is a *tour de force* in a
matter in which, up to that, he has never shown any interest;
it is commonly thought to be the preserve of his rival,
George Colley. This will surely push him a notch or two
higher to the top of the ladder—a direction in which he is
clearly headed.

When it is all over, he takes me out on to the veranda
behind the house, looking over the rich pastureland. And
there, lo and behold, the cold, calculating hooded eyes light
up with glee and I see a sight I never expected to see: the
Minister for Finance dances up and down the veranda with
delight, a very Pied Piper of Hamelin charmed by the impact
he has clearly made.

Incidentally, it is in the course of that interview that he
first announces the tax-free concession to artists. He had
been to Mass earlier in the local church in Kinsealy, he says,
and, looking at the appalling plaster statues around the walls,
the idea came to him that if Irish sculptors and artists were
properly endowed, they could surely do better work than
that. But how to endow them, that was the question? So the
idea of the tax-free concession was born, an idea from which
many writers and artists have benefited since—some, be it
said, who returned the compliment by biting the hand that
fed them! 'Ingratitude, thou marble-hearted friend!' King
Lear might have had a point.

It had, as I say, been something of a surprise that day to
hear how sincere he sounded about the language. Then he
suddenly tells us that we are not to be too impressed with all
that; hadn't it always been so with politicians—full of plans
and promises, but when it came to implementation, little or
nothing was done? It seemed to be permanently a case of

hell being paved with good intentions. It would not be so with him: in any ministry he had ever been in, he had done what he said he would do—the motto of the old Fianna warriors, 'Beart do réir do bhriathair'. But then he adds this revealing rider: 'I can do nothing really comprehensive until I am Taoiseach.'

Not alone will it be a long time before he becomes Taoiseach, it will be a long time before he becomes anything else at all. Following his sacking during the Arms Crisis in 1970, he becomes a displaced person, very much out in the cold. But he still manages to retain the grand seigneur style, one aspect of which is an insouciant strut, which seems to say that however little others may think of him, he is in no doubt about what he thinks of himself.

It is with this strut that he moves through the company on a May day in 1971 when the all-Irish school Scoil Neasáin in Raheny is being blessed. The blessing is performed by the newly appointed Auxiliary Bishop of Dublin, one James Kavanagh, a decent man and a Dubliner to the core—his father before him had been involved with the Dublin football team. It so happens that I am in conversation with Bishop Kavanagh after the event when Charles J. comes towards us. The initial pleasantries are exchanged (the conversation is in Irish) and I ask him if he is coming into the reception for a cup of coffee or tea afterwards. 'Tae nó caifé, Ó Murchú?' comes the lofty reproof, 'Champagne an t-aon deoch amháin roimh am lóin!'—an early echo of sounds that will recur in distant times to come!

The native argot of these two quintessential Dubliners is not, however, to be long denied. Both are ex-Christian Brothers boys, one from the working-class O'Connell

School in North Richmond Street, the other from the even more aggressively working-class Joey's in Marino. Such folk speak to each other in a language all their own.

'What in the name of God, Ó Murchú,' Charlie eventually asks, 'is the Irish hierarchy coming to when they make Jimmy Kavanagh a bishop?'

It is a question to which I have no easy answer. Even if I had, I would have been too speechless to come out with it. But not so his purple-cassocked fellow Dubliner. Drawing evenly on his pipe, his response, when it comes, leaves me more speechless still.

'Ah yes, Charlie. And the difference between me and you is that I intend to remain one!'

Whatever about the sincerity of Haughey's attitudes to other aspects of the national life, there could never be any doubting the genuineness of his admiration for Seán Ó Riada. *Mise Éire* (1959) and *Saoirse* (1961) had come at a crucial point in the graph of his own rise to fame; it was also a time when a dynamic new drive for economic expansion had been launched, heralded by T. K. Whitaker's 'First Programme for Economic Development'. Ó Riada himself was quite partial to the idea of the rich patron—in his case nowhere better exemplified than in the great musical nights with his Ceoltóirí Chualann in Luggala House in County Wicklow under the patronage of the Guinness scion, Garech de Brún. So, when Ó Riada comes up from Cúil Aodha for a 'last hurrah' with the Ceoltóirí in the Gaiety, it is no surprise that Charles should come along with a goodly retinue of his rich and powerful friends. A great night's music and celebration is had by all, most memorable for Ó Riada's re-creation of the lovely airs of Bunting: 'Marbhna Luimní', 'An Ghaoth

Aneas', 'Mná na hÉireann'. This is around the time that Ó Riada has discovered Ballyferriter and the house of sean nós singer, Seán de hÓra, above Clochar beach, looking out over the Blaskets—upon which, as we know, Charles Haughey soon sets an eye to build a holiday home on the island of Inishvikallane.

From then on, during the summer months, a not unfamiliar sight is the helicopter dropping out of the sky in a field beside Kruger Kavanagh's pub in Dún Chaoin. Fianna Fáil are back in government; Jack Lynch is back as Taoiseach; Haughey is back as Minister for Health and Social Welfare. In my role as Cathaoirleach of Bord na Gaeilge, I am trying to give effect to some of the things we had talked about in his years as Minister for Finance, one of which was to get more of a presence for Irish in the public services. It is with this in mind that I go to see him one day in the summer of 1978. He is late arriving in the office in Áras MhicDhiarmada but, when eventually he does come, I cannot help noticing how well he looks.

'Just in from Innishvikallane,' he tells me. 'Dublin for the football, Kerry for the holidays! Your friend, Ó Riada, made no mistake when he told me to get a place down there.'

It is a sentiment which he would repeat—this time tragically at Ó Riada's funeral in Baile Bhúirne. Around him that day were Willie Clancy, the piper from Milltown Malbay, sean nós singer Seán Mac Donncha from Cárna, John Kelly from Belfast, sculptor Séamus Murphy of *Stone Mad*, General Tom Barry of *Guerilla Days in Ireland* and myself from Cork. All of us, with the thousands of others that day, were equally touched with profound respect for what Ó Riada had done for the culture and self-esteem of Ireland. But none more so, let it be said at this later time of trauma in his life, than Charles Haughey who, incidentally, would not be remiss in seeing to it that Seán's family would have a friend to call on in the troubled times ahead.

His convincing apologia for the language in the 'Watch Your Language' interview did not come to an end with his tenure in Finance. Close on ten years later, while Minister for Health and Social Welfare in Jack Lynch's government, I walk in on him one night in make-up in RTÉ, where he is being prepared for a promotional piece on an upcoming marathon run sponsored by the Health Education Bureau. This is part of a new national 'Keep Fit and Avoid Illness' drive—the sort of approach which has become widespread now but was a novel idea then. Its basis, 'prevention is better than cure', was at once logical and publicly appealing. With my Bord na Gaeilge hat on, I had a very lively interest in trying to do things in a way that would be publicly appealing, things which would lift the language out of the rut of old-established, largely failed rituals of rules, regulations and curricular compulsions into an atmosphere where people would want to learn and speak it for its own sake and for the love of it.

'When I'm Taoiseach,' I tell him, 'not if, but when, the first thing I'll do is make you Minister for the Gaeltacht.'

'Why would you do that now?'

'Because you'd make real things happen, like what you're doing now with Health.' As I knew only too well from my own time there, the emphasis in Health was always on hospitals, buildings, drugs and expensive medicines—all aimed at curing illness rather than preventing it. 'You're only a short while in the job and already you have the whole country running around the roads at night keeping fit. That's the kind of kick-start the Irish language needs, and you are the man to give it.'

This light-hearted conversation took place in the RTÉ

make-up room on a night in 1978. A short time later, Charles J. does indeed become Taoiseach and, through the agency of his good friend and close adviser, Pádraig Ó hAnnracháin, I get the opportunity to remind him of that conversation and of the point I then made. His response is testy, monosyllabic—the familiar growl is still there. He is a busy man, trying to put together enough support from among the independents to form a government; the language is about the last thing on his mind. So I do not take offence when he puts down the phone in a manner which suggests that that is the last I will hear of it. It is not. The following day, when he becomes Taoiseach, he adds to his portfolio one further task, that of Minister for the Gaeltacht as well. Maybe in that light-hearted exchange in RTÉ he *was* listening after all!

From first to last, the language continues to be central to the contacts I have with him. There will be one further such contact before he finally leaves: that is in the run-up to the General Election of 1987, when I get a phone call from his private secretary, Catherine Butler, asking me to come and see him. About what, I ask, but Catherine does not know; she will however enquire. The phone goes dead for a time while she does; when it comes alive, it is with that old familiar growl: 'Don't be asking stupid questions, Ó Murchú. Just get down here as soon as you can. I'll tell you then.' Nevertheless, I persist; if he will give me some idea, I may be able to have some response ready, to save us all time.

'It's policy papers for the Manifesto,' I am told. 'First the language, and if you have any ideas on broadcasting, you can think about that too.'

Experience with drafting Committee and Report Stage notes has taught me to think fast on such matters, and to write even faster. When I meet him an hour later, I have the outlines of what I think should go into such policy papers; these I read over to him while we sit there drinking tea from an exquisite china tea-set. The language paper is written partly in Irish; so I politely ask if he will be able to follow it. The growl tells me I have touched on a sore point: how dare a Christian Brothers boy from the mere North Mon. of Cork put it to a Christian Brothers Dub from the superior Joey's of Marino that Irish is a language he cannot understand!

'I want you to make two additions to it,' he tells me when I have finished. 'First, something favourable about the Gaelscoileanna, the all-Irish schools, and, second, something strong and favourable about Telefís na Gaeilge.'

Having thought long and hard about this Telefís na Gaeilge, I had come to the view that the most advantageous approach for the language would not be a separate service at all which, even at its best, could never hope to reach a sizeable segment of the viewing public, but to get a dedicated period of time, two/three hours a night, on RTÉ's Network 2. In that way audiences would stand a chance of being maintained and the danger of ghettoising the language would be avoided. But Haughey was adamant: he wanted a clear commitment made in that policy statement that a separate Irish language service would be set up. It was, I believe, the first unequivocal governmental commitment to the idea.

What this conversation led on to in due course was membership of an election think-tank, a diverse and talented group of people, including P. J. O'Mara, Martin Mansergh, Seamus Brennan, Brendan O'Kelly, Fred O'Donovan, Paul Kavanagh and PR man Tom Savage. The 7.30 morning meetings were bright and lively affairs, especially when

Charles J. himself turned up to inject some extra shots of life into them. It was at these meetings, and specifically from him, that we first heard some names that would make an important impact upon the economic life of Ireland: Dermot Desmond, the man behind the now hugely successful Financial Services Centre, and Professor Gerry Wrixon, now President of UCC and a major influence in the phenomenal growth of the computer industry.

But elections are about winning—about losing too—and a crucial item in the run-up to election time is what RTÉ was pleased to call 'The Great Debate'. This face-to-face between then Taoiseach Garret FitzGerald and Charles Haughey is an eagerly awaited event, in which all concerned expect Haughey to weigh into FitzGerald with the heavy armour he has at his disposal: chronic unemployment, lengthening dole queues, rising emigration—in a word, to visit upon him some of the *saeva indignatio* the public is feeling at the rudderless way the country is being run. Instead, what we get is a cool, calm and collected Charles Haughey, a model of restraint and good reason, not at all a man so perturbed about the current state of things that he is likely to do anything radical to arrest it. Meanwhile, Garret, the statistician, dances about him with the pyrotechnics of his trade—to us viewers a highly convincing performance.

The following morning, when we assemble to review matters, it is uniformly agreed that Haughey has lost the round. The debate has gone Garret's way; and unless something urgent can be done to redress matters, such electoral support as might be gained from the occasion is lost.

There is just one further slim chance: the half-hour radio interview following the Main News on Sunday. It is generally agreed that Haughey will have to change his tune dramatically for that. The polite, restrained, even-tempered Charles Haughey of 'The Great Debate' will have done little or nothing to convince distracted mothers and fathers that their sons and daughters will ever find jobs in Ireland; even less to reassure those in jobs that they won't soon be out of them, getting redundancy payments and joining the dole queues—or, worse still, heading down the quays for the emigrant ship or out to Dublin, Shannon or Cork airports for the London and New York/Boston flights. Whoever was going to turn all that around would have to take the economy by the scruff of the neck and make things happen; for that, he would have to make a far stronger, more impassioned plea.

I undertake to get all this into one short, single-page note which will be passed to him before the interview. Several of the group read and approve that note, but Martin Mansergh in particular, astute and diplomatic man that he is, thinks it a shade too sharp, too critical of his television performance. Perhaps, I am advised, it would be best if I deliver it myself. In favour of those who so advise me, I must allow that I am not as aware as they are of the man's fabled wrath with messengers bearing bad news!

I bide my time, hoping that something will transpire which will alter the state of things and obviate the need to send this note of mine at all. Nothing does. So, it is Saturday and it still has not gone. Will I send it? Won't I? The broadcast will be the following day. Not even the customary curmudgeonly growl greets me when I finally decide to take my courage in my hands and deliver the dread message. I read rapidly through the page; there is no response from the far end, nothing but silence; it is not a friendly silence. I begin to see why the scholarly Mansergh suggested that the messenger do the delivering himself!

'That all?' are the sole words that reach me when I have finished. They are followed by a peremptory 'Thanks', and the phone goes down. It seems a poor price for my pains.

But the following day, it is a very different Charles Haughey who takes to the air-waves: an angry, aggressive man, full of that *saeva indignatio* we all knew was there but had not been expressed, someone acutely aware of the state of things and full of resolve to change it.

The economists and statisticians will have their own say on all this; but, in this groundling's view, if we have a Celtic Tiger among us in these years, it is from around that time that the first signs of its arrival may be dated.

Those of us who saw Ireland beat England in the final game of the Triple Crown in 1985 will not easily forget team captain, Ciarán Fitzgerald, mouthing his rugged challenge to his mud-covered forwards in the final minutes. With the wild clamour all about him, one could not actually hear what he said—but, caught in full frontal on camera, there was no doubting the lip-synch with which he said it: 'Where's your fucking pride?' That night, after the leader's speech at the Fianna Fáil Ard-Fheis in the Royal Dublin Society, Haughey came into the press gallery, where the usual crowd of journalists and media folk were gathered for the bread-and-circuses that are part and parcel of all such events. When, briefly, our paths crossed, I asked him if he had seen the game earlier in the day. Yes, he said, and he had also heard what Ciarán Fitzgerald had said.

'What that was in plain English,' he told me, 'was— "Múscail do mhisneach!"'

It is a phrase which, in more recent times, Charles

Haughey will have had good reason to remember. There has certainly been enough in the sordid scandal of his financial affairs and his personal life to crush any man's spirit. That he manages to survive and still come out in public is indeed extraordinary. By normal standards, he is an old man now, with his deeds and misdeeds behind him. Granting for a moment that the Celtic Tiger prosperity we now enjoy owes some part of its origins to him, this much may at least be said: there must be thousands of emigrants, young and not so young, whose 'Come back to Erin' call would not have happened but for the opportunities his policies opened up; and thousands more in jobs now who would not be in them but for the thrust and drive they brought to Irish commercial life. A thriving economy, a huge budgetary surplus, the national debt dropping, a growing workforce which not all that long ago would have been under threat of redundancy and the dole—some at least of that started with him. What has recently come to light about his own 'take' from all that is indeed a cause of scandal, even criminal perhaps—at the time of writing it is too soon to say. But what must not be denied is that earlier record of achievement, one that enabled him to say, with Othello, on the day he finally left public office: 'I have done the state some service.'

What then of the matter which some regard as the most flagrant in the category of his many misdeeds: his affair with a tactless woman and his unfaithfulness to a good and decent wife? Those among the prurient public who would stone him for that ought to be careful not to cast the first stone. Perhaps the most significant feature of it is the fact that the person most entitled to blame him has never once done so. Her loyalty—that of their family too—may in some small measure be a lesson to all finger-wagging moralists in these loose and free-fall times.

Finally, since much of the commentary in these pages is about matters associated with the language, and since my personal association with Charles Haughey over the years was mostly to do with the language too, I like to think that his interpretation of that challenge of Ciarán Fitzgerald on Triple Crown day 1985 should now, more than ever, have a significance in the language's future and its life. In each of the two millennia the nation has passed through, it was the one abiding mark of our nationhood. That it has survived to a third, despite constant efforts to bury it, is surely a proof that the survivor instinct is intact. To progress from here will indeed require much dedication, courage and hard work. For that, what better rallying cry than that of those starry-eyed nation-dreamers at the turn of the nineteenth century: 'Múscail do mhisneach, a Bhanba!'